Balloon View Publishing Ltd
145 Littlestone Road
New Romney
Kent, TN28 8NH

www.balloonview.com

ISBN 978-1-907798-92-4

Printed in the United Kingdom for Balloon View Publishing Ltd by Short Run Press, Exeter, Devon, UK.

A CIP Catalogue record for this book is available from the British Library.

ABOUT THE AUTHOR

Edward Peppitt is a publishing consultant, trainer, and writer with over 30 years' experience in both traditional and self-publishing. He began his career in educational publishing, serving as Publishing Director at Letts Educational, and has since worked with many of the UK's leading publishers, including Emap, Hodder, Channel 4, HarperCollins, Oxford University Press, and Cambridge University Press.

As a publishing trainer, Ed supports authors at every stage of their publishing journey — from first-time writers to established experts — providing practical advice, hands-on training and production guidance. He has taught the popular Guardian self-publishing weekend masterclass for several years, spoken at countless industry events, and hosted industry podcasts on business, technology and publishing topics.

Ed is also the author of seven business and computing books, as well as The Beacon Bike — an account of his 3,500-mile cycle ride around the UK coast visiting every onshore and offshore lighthouse. He lives on the Kent coast with his family and two dogs, and remains mildly obsessed with lighthouses, good books, and cricket.

THE SELF-PUBLISHING PLAYBOOK

CLEAR, HONEST ADVICE FOR AUTHORS WHO
WANT CONTROL (NOT FALSE PROMISES)

EDWARD PEPPITT

BALLOONVIEW
PUBLISHING

CONTENTS

READY TO REALLY GET STARTED?

Reading this book is a brilliant start, but publishing your book doesn't happen on paper alone.

If you'd like step-by-step help to publish your book sooner (and with fewer headaches), join me for my online Self-Publishing training programme, delivered online LIVE over five afternoons.

- Live, practical sessions — not pre-recorded videos.
- No jargon, no false promises — just honest guidance from a publishing sector expert.
- Small group support — Maximum of 12 writers on each course.
- Walk away with a clear plan, ready to publish.

Book readers get a special bonus: When you join from this book, you'll also receive my exclusive companion workbook to help you put every lesson into action.

Find out more and secure your place at:
www.getpublished.tv/courses/self-publish-properly

I can't wait to help you make your book a reality.

Ed.

INTRODUCTION

Publishing a book can stir up all sorts of emotions—many of them unexpected.

You might feel excited. You might feel exposed. You might even feel a little bit lost, especially once the writing stops and the waiting begins. That's perfectly normal.

This introduction isn't about the nuts and bolts of self-publishing. It's about mindset. Before considering the steps to take to publish your book, it is helpful to understand how becoming an author can impact your confidence, motivation, and sense of self.

What's your reason for publishing?

Every author has their reason. Some want to build a platform. Some want to share their experience. Some want to hold a finished book in their hands.

None of these reasons is wrong, but it's essential to be honest with yourself about yours. If your goal is to make money, your decisions about editing, marketing and pricing will look very different from someone who's writing for family and friends.

By being clear from the start, you'll avoid chasing someone else's definition of success.

Publishing is personal

Even if your book is about a practical subject, it still comes from you. Your voice. Your choices. Your effort.

That's why publishing can feel oddly exposing, especially when the first reviews come in. You might find yourself reading between the lines, looking for signs of approval, or worrying about whether you're being taken seriously.

The truth is that most people will be glad you've written something. They'll admire the fact you've stuck with it and that you've dared to put your work out there.

The comparison trap

It's easy to feel like everyone else is doing better. Other authors seem to have bigger launches, glossier covers, and more sales.

But don't forget: the only stories we tend to hear are the success stories. We don't see the false starts, the failed edits, the books that quietly disappear.

Your journey doesn't have to look like anyone else's. Focus

on your book, your readers, and your goals. That's more than enough.

From Writer to Author

There's a quiet shift that happens when you go from writing a book to preparing to publish it. You're no longer just a writer—you're an author. That means thinking not just about the words on the page, but about your reader.

This mindset shift is decisive. When you view yourself as an author, you start making more informed decisions about your book, process, and goals. You stop asking "Is this good enough?" and start asking "Does this do justice to the story I want to tell?"

When the excitement fades

Many authors experience a dip in motivation after their book is published. You spend months working towards the big day, and then it comes and goes. The buzz fades, and you're left wondering what's next.

This is common. Don't panic. Take a breath. Give your book time to find its readers. And if you're already thinking about the next one, that's a good sign.

Activity: Your publishing goals

Take a moment to jot down your personal goals for publishing this book. Be honest.

- Why do I want to publish this book?
- What does success look like to me?

- Who am I writing it for?
- What would I be proud to achieve?

Refer back to this later, especially if you hit a dip. It will remind you why you started—and what matters.

1

DEBUNKING THE MYTHS

The decision to self-publish is exciting and motivating, as long as you are making it for the right reasons. Self-publishing has advanced so much over the last few years. With the many tools, applications and platforms to help, it's easier than ever before to bring your story or message to life in a professionally published format.

Nevertheless, the route is strewn with myths, misleading ideas and polarised views spread by well-meaning amateurs, self-proclaimed experts, and predatory companies looking to profit from new authors like you.

This chapter addresses the most common misconceptions about self-publishing, replacing them with practical and empowering truths to guide you on your journey.

Myth 1: AI Can Write and Publish Your Bestseller

The Myth: Artificial intelligence tools are so advanced that they can write a bestseller – in any genre - with minimal input from you. Just input a prompt, and the AI will generate a flawless manuscript ready for publication.

The Reality: Before we even consider whether this claim is valid, you should ask yourself why you'd want AI to write your book for you. Aren't you a writer who is looking to get published? If you're happy to leave the writing to an AI application, then I would question your motive for wanting to see it published.

AI tools are incredible for brainstorming, researching, drafting, and refining, but they lack the creativity, emotional depth, and nuanced storytelling that make a book stand out. While AI can provide inspiration or polish your prose, it cannot replicate the unique voice and perspective that only you can bring to your work. Books written entirely by AI often feel flat, generic, and disconnected, which is why successful authors use AI as an assistant, not a replacement.

Takeaway: Use AI to assist, not to automate, your publishing journey.

Myth 2: Self-Publishing is Quick and Effortless

The Myth: Self-publishing is a straightforward process that requires only a few clicks. Once you've uploaded your manuscript to a platform like Amazon's KDP (Kindle Direct Publishing), you'll instantly start seeing sales roll in.

The Reality: This myth is based on a misunderstanding about what publishing involves. There's a lot more to it than simply uploading a manuscript. It requires careful preparation, including editing, typesetting, indexing, proofreading, designing a professional cover, and developing a marketing plan. Each of these steps requires time, effort, and a financial investment. Self-publishing success comes from treating it as a professional endeavour and committing to quality at every stage.

Takeaway: Approach self-publishing as a project that requires planning, effort, patience and investment.

Myth 3: You Need to Pay Thousands to Publish Your Book

The Myth: Unless you invest heavily in services like editing, design, and distribution, your self-published book will fail. Some 'self-publishing companies' claim that spending thousands on their bundled publishing services is the only way to ensure success.

The Reality: While there are costs associated with self-publishing, they don't have to break the bank. Many affordable freelancers, platforms, and tools can help you create a professional-quality book within a reasonable budget. Nearly half of the editors, typesetters and cover designers who work for mainstream publishers are freelancers, who would work for you as readily as they would work for them. So you can scale your investment based on your goals without overspending on unnecessary extras.

Takeaway: Be cautious of companies selling overpriced publishing 'packages' that often deliver poor value.

Myth 4: You'll Earn Passive Income Overnight

The Myth: Publishing your book is like planting a money tree—you'll sit back and watch the royalties roll in effortlessly.

The Reality: Selling books requires consistent marketing and audience-building to succeed. Even a brilliantly written book can go unnoticed without proper promotion. Successful self-published authors connect and engage with their readers through social media, email campaigns, and partnerships. They invest time in building their brand and understanding their audience's preferences. Passive income is possible, but only after you put in the work to make your book visible. And let's be clear, only a tiny percentage of published books make substantial, income-replacing royalties for their authors.

Takeaway: Consider your book as a product that requires an effective marketing strategy.

Myth 5: The Promise of Instant Success

The Myth: Some companies promise to make you a bestseller—guaranteed. Others claim to have a "foolproof" publishing system, if you're willing to invest thousands upfront.

The Reality: Be cautious. No reputable publishing service can guarantee a specific number of sales, chart success, or glowing reviews. What they *can* offer is quality editing, professional production, and realistic advice about your book's potential.

Takeaway: Always ask questions. What exactly am I paying for? Who will be doing the work? Do I keep the rights to my book? If you feel rushed to sign or unclear about the deliverables, walk away.

Myth 6: Bookstores Won't Stock Self-Published Books

The Myth: If you self-publish, traditional bookstores will automatically reject your book because it doesn't come from a recognised publisher.

The Reality: While traditional high street bookshops tend to favour established publishers, many local and independent booksellers are open to self-published books that meet professional quality standards. The key is to ensure your book is visible, easily accessible, and available quickly at attractive trade terms. Building relationships with bookshop owners and offering bulk deals can also increase your chances of success.

Takeaway: Focus on creating a professional-quality book and building relationships with local and independent booksellers.

Myth 7: You Don't Need Professional Editing

The Myth: A quick spell check or grammar check is enough to polish your manuscript for publication. Grammarly will do all the heavy lifting for you.

The Reality: Professional editing is crucial for producing a high-quality book that readers can take seriously. Editors not only catch errors that automated tools might miss but also improve the structure, clarity, and flow of your manuscript. A professionally edited book is more likely to receive positive reviews, which can significantly impact its success. Skipping this step is one of the most common mistakes self-published authors make.

The professional editing myth is based on a misunderstanding of what editing entails. For those who perpetuate the myth, editing is nothing more than spell-checking and proofreading. We will consider what editing involves in a later chapter.

Takeaway: Editing is an investment, not a luxury. Please don't skip it.

Myth 8: Self-Published Books Can't Be Bestsellers

The Myth: Only traditionally published books achieve bestseller status or significant sales.

The Reality: Many self-published authors have achieved bestseller status by targeting specific niches and employing effective marketing strategies. For example, Andy Weir's *The Martian* and E.L. James's *Fifty Shades of Grey* both started as self-published books before becoming international phenomena. With platforms like Amazon and social media, authors can connect directly with their audience and achieve remarkable success.

Takeaway: Success depends on your strategy, not your publishing route.

Myth 9: Your Book Will Look Amateur Without a Traditional Publisher

The Myth: Self-published books are automatically low-quality and unprofessional compared to traditionally published ones.

The Reality: A decade ago, it was easy to identify a self-published book. The paper type, print quality and cover card stock available to self-published authors didn't match the quality that a mainstream publisher could depend on.

Things are very different today. At a publishing training session last year, I took a handful of books with me, some self-published and some published traditionally. Only a few people could differentiate between them. With access to new publishing tools, freelance professionals and modern digital printing presses, self-published books look better than ever.

Takeaway: Prioritise quality in every aspect of your book's production.

Myth 10: Print-on-Demand is Too Expensive for Self-Published Authors

The Myth: Print-on-demand (POD) books are so costly that you'll never make a profit.

The Reality: Print-on-demand (POD) is an efficient solution for authors who prefer not to invest in large print runs of their book. As the name suggests, a copy of your book is only printed once a sale has been made. While the cost per unit is higher than bulk printing, POD eliminates the risk of unsold inventory. It's ideal for testing demand or printing tiny quantities. Many successful self-published authors use POD to fulfil orders directly through platforms like Amazon.

Takeaway: Use POD strategically, especially when starting out or testing demand.

Myth 11: You Don't Need a Marketing Plan

The Myth: A good book will sell itself through word-of-mouth.

The Reality: Every successful author I have encountered has invested time and effort into marketing their book. Whether planning a launch strategy, engaging on social media or building an audience, they have understood the importance of marketing and promotion in driving sales. Without a marketing plan, even the best-written books risk being lost in a crowded market. Successful marketing doesn't just happen—it's planned and executed.

Takeaway: A strong marketing plan is as essential as the book itself.

Myth 12: The More Publishing Services You Buy, the Better Your Book Will Be

The Myth: Paying for every available self-publishing service guarantees success.

The Reality: So-called 'self-publishing companies' tend to provide a vast range of add-on services. Not all are necessary or valuable. While editing, cover design, typesetting, and marketing are essential, many self-publishing packages bundle unnecessary extras that add little to no additional value. Authors should evaluate each service carefully and prioritise those that genuinely enhance their book's quality or reach.

Takeaway: Be strategic with your investments and focus on the essentials.

Myth 13: Self-Publishing is a One-Shot Process

The Myth: Once your book is published, your work is finished.

The Reality: Publishing is just the beginning. Successful self-publishing involves ongoing marketing, interacting with readers, and sometimes revising or updating your work. The journey doesn't end with publication; it's a continual process of growth and engagement.

Takeaway: Consider publishing as the beginning of a long-term journey, not the end.

Myth 14: Hybrid or Collaborative Publishing Means Shared Risk

The Myth: Some publishing companies present themselves as "hybrid" or "collaborative" publishers, claiming to share the cost of publishing with the author. They suggest that by investing in your book, they're entering into a partnership with you where you both contribute financially and benefit equally from the outcome. On the surface, this can sound appealing, like a middle ground between traditional publishing and self-publishing.

The Reality: In practice, many so-called hybrid or collaborative publishers do not genuinely share the costs or risks associated with your book. Instead, they inflate the prices of editorial, design, and production services—often charging authors two or three times what those same services would cost independently. That means when they 'split' the costs with you, you're still paying as much as if you had commissioned each service yourself. The promise of *shared investment* is therefore misleading, and you are also giving away a proportion of your royalties or income unnecessarily.

Another potential downside to working with a hybrid or collaborative publisher is that they often rely solely on print-on-demand sales. That will make each copy you buy yourself more expensive, and may also limit your book's sales potential in high street retailers like Waterstones or WH Smith.

Although some hybrid publishers operate ethically and transparently, many prioritise their financial gain over a book's success once payment from the author has been received.

Takeaway: Always scrutinise the fine print. If a publisher asks you to pay, make sure you're getting genuine value—compare their services with freelancers or self-publishing platforms, and don't be misled by language like "shared investment." In most cases, you'll get a better deal—and retain more control—by hiring trusted professionals directly.

Myth 15: Publishing is Easy Money – Just Follow My Proven System

The Myth: Social media is full of "publishing gurus" and skillfully promoted systems that promise effortless success. They claim you can make thousands, sometimes tens of thousands, by turning your expertise into published books. For just a small fee, they'll reveal the secret method.

The Reality: Most of these offers are either dramatically oversold or outright exploitative. The low-cost, high-reward claims *"Get paid $5,000 for eBooks you didn't write"* prey on people's hopes for passive income, but they rarely deliver. The business models behind them typically rely on volume, low quality, and misleading advertising.

These companies profit by positioning authorship as a get-rich-quick scheme or a turnkey status symbol, not a creative or professional endeavour. They are rarely the complete solution they promise to be, and certainly don't replace the need for strategy, structure, and original thought.

Takeaway: If something sounds too good to be true, it probably is. Real publishing success takes time, thought, effort, and care. Be especially wary of anyone who:

- Guarantees income or bestseller status.
- Says you don't need to write or be involved in the book's content.
- Charges luxury-level fees without transparency about deliverables.

Always ask: *Who benefits here?* If it's not the reader—and it's not you—then it's probably a confidence trick wearing a publishing badge.

Myth 16: You Should Sell Direct — Keep More Money and Own Your Audience

The Myth: Some publishing platforms and marketing gurus claim that selling your books directly, through your website or custom-built bookstore, is the smart, modern way to publish. They argue that by cutting out retailers like Amazon, you'll keep a bigger share of the profits, gain direct access to your customers, and build a loyal readership that you control. On paper, it sounds like an entrepreneurial dream: total ownership, total margin, total freedom.

The Reality: You will indeed earn more money from selling a copy of your book directly to a customer than from selling it on Amazon. However, while selling directly avoids retailer margins and provides valuable customer data, this claim massively underestimates the effort involved in changing reader behaviour. The vast majority of readers don't want to visit multiple authors' websites to buy books. They shop on Amazon (and other major retailers) because it's fast, familiar, trusted, and frictionless. With just a couple of taps, they can buy and start reading —especially on Kindle, which dominates the eBook market.

When you ask readers to purchase directly, you're asking them to change a deeply ingrained habit—and to do something that is, in most cases, less convenient. For print books, readers might hesitate to enter credit card details on a site they've never heard of. For eBooks, the challenge is even greater. Getting a non-Kindle eBook file (such as an EPUB or PDF) onto a Kindle device can be fiddly, inconsistent, and off-putting for most people. And if your reader doesn't enjoy a smooth reading experience, they may not come back.

As for "owning your audience," it's certainly beneficial to have a mailing list and direct relationship with your readers. But building that audience takes time, trust, and repeated value, not just a buy button on your website. Amazon takes a significant cut for a reason: it offers discoverability, convenience, and conversion. It delivers customers to your book.

Takeaway: Selling directly can be part of your long-term strategy, but it works best when you already have a loyal audience, rather than as a substitute for the reach and trust that retailers provide. Think of it as *complementary*, not *foundational*. If you're starting, your time and energy are usually better spent making your book easy to find and buy on the platforms readers already use.

Red Flags: How to Spot a Predatory Publisher

- They promise you'll be a bestseller.
- They charge hefty upfront fees but don't explain what you're paying for.
- They use high-pressure sales tactics.
- They say editing isn't necessary if you use their "system."
- They won't let you retain full rights to your book.

If it sounds too good to be true, it usually is. Self-publishing doesn't mean going it alone—but you do need to choose your partners wisely.

The Realities of Self-Publishing

1. **It's a Journey:** Self-publishing requires learning, effort, patience and persistence.
2. **Quality Counts:** Professionalism in editing, design, and typesetting is essential.
3. **You're in Control:** The rewards of self-publishing come from taking ownership of the process.

Practical Checklist

- Identify and dismiss myths that have held you back.
- Embrace the effort required to self-publish professionally.

- Start thinking of self-publishing as a business endeavour.

The truth about self-publishing is more empowering than the myths surrounding it. It's a path that demands effort, but with the right approach, it offers incredible opportunities. In the next chapter, we'll discuss scoping your writing project before you start writing.

2

SCOPING YOUR PROJECT – BEFORE YOU START WRITING

You may be eager to begin writing. Or you might already have 20,000 words stashed away on your laptop. Either way, before you go any further, it's worth stopping to ask yourself a few big-picture questions.

That's because publishing a book isn't just about the words on the page. It's about what you want the book to do—who it's for, how it will be used, and where it will be sold. If you can get clear on that now, you'll save yourself a lot of time, money and second-guessing later on.

This chapter gives you a simple framework for defining your book's purpose, structure and audience—before you dive too deep.

Start with "Why"

Before you start planning your content, think about your deeper motivation. Why are you writing this book? Is it to share a story? Build a profile? Help a specific group of people? Capture something important before it's lost?

This kind of reflection isn't just sentimental—it's strategic. Your purpose will shape how you write, who you write for, and what you consider a successful outcome. If your goal is to make an impact, you'll write differently than if your goal is income or legacy. So, please take a moment to pause and reflect.

What type of book are you writing?

This might sound obvious, but it isn't always. Your book might be a practical guide, a memoir, a short manifesto, a collection of poetry, or something hybrid. Defining the type of book early on will influence:

- Its length and tone
- Its visual design and page layout
- How readers will find and use it

Think about what your reader will expect from this kind of book—and how you'll deliver it.

Who is it for?

This is crucial. Your book is not for everyone. The more precisely you can define your reader, the more powerful and helpful your writing will become.

Ask yourself:

- What do they already know?
- What do they want to learn, feel or experience?

- What would make them pick up this book over others?

Picture your reader as an individual, not a crowd. It makes your writing more focused—and your marketing easier.

How will readers find it?

This question is often skipped, but it matters.

Will your book primarily be available on Amazon? Will you sell it at talks, or hand it out at events? Will it be read by clients or by strangers? These decisions affect how you title your book, design the cover, write the blurb, and more.

It's hard to get this right at the end. It's much easier if you start thinking about it now.

What Does Success Look Like?

It helps to define what success means for you, right now. That could be selling 1,000 copies, or using your book to secure speaking gigs, or giving a copy to each member of your family. There's no correct answer—only the one that makes this project worthwhile to *you*.

When you know what you're aiming for, it becomes easier to make decisions about length, tone, budget, and format. And when things get hard (as they sometimes will), it gives you something solid to return to.

Caution: Common Pitfalls

- Writing for "everyone" instead of a specific reader.
- Aiming for overnight success without a plan.

- Thinking the book will sell itself.
- Choosing style over substance—or vice versa.

A bit of planning now can save you a lot of frustration later. Start with clarity.

Activity: Scoping Checklist

Here's a quick planning checklist to help you clarify your project before you write another word:

Make notes on each of the following:

- What kind of book am I writing?
- Who is my reader?
- What do they want from this book?
- What outcome am I hoping for?
- How will I use or distribute the book?
- What tone or voice do I want to use?
- What does success look like to me?

You don't need to have perfect answers to every question. But even rough ideas will help shape your thinking—and prevent major detours later on.

In the next chapter, we will consider the purpose of publishing your book in more detail.

3

THE PURPOSE OF PUBLISHING YOUR BOOK

Why do you want to publish a book? It's a simple question, but one that often prompts varied and even profound answers. For some, publishing is a profoundly personal achievement—a way to share a story, honour a memory, or fulfil a lifelong dream. For others, it's a strategic move—a tool to establish expertise, build credibility, or promote a business. Whatever your reasons, understanding your purpose is critical to guiding your publishing journey.

This chapter will help you explore your "why" and demonstrate how a book can elevate your personal or professional profile, open doors, and create a lasting impact.

Why Publish a Book?

Publishing a book is about more than just putting words on paper. It's about creating a tangible product that represents your storytelling ability, creativity, knowledge, and ideas. Here are some of the key reasons people choose to publish:

1. Establish Credibility

A published book positions you as an authority in your field. Whether you're a consultant, business owner, or thought leader, having a book to your name signals expertise and commitment. After all, the phrase "author" shares its root with "authority" for a reason.

2. Build Visibility

Books are powerful tools for increasing your online and offline presence. A book listed on Amazon, for example, increases your searchability, while physical copies at events or in bookstores extend your reach.

3. Tell Your Story

For many, writing a book is a deeply personal journey—a chance to document experiences, share lessons learned, or inspire others. Memoirs and individual stories have a unique ability to connect with readers at an emotional level.

4. Generate Income and Opportunities

While few authors are fortunate enough to rely solely on book sales for their income, a book can open doors to new opportunities. Speaking engagements, consulting projects, or even coaching programs can stem from the credibility a book provides.

Publishing for Legacy, Family or Community

Not every book is written with commercial success in mind. Some are written to preserve memories, share personal experiences, or pass something meaningful to the next generation.

You might be documenting a family history, a personal health journey, a collection of wartime letters, or the story of a local organisation. These books often have a small, specific audience, but that doesn't make them any less valuable. They may be the most important books you've ever written.

We sometimes refer to this as legacy publishing—creating a book to commemorate a life, a place, or a moment in time. These projects aren't about sales rankings or Amazon reviews. They're about recording, honouring, and sharing.

And self-publishing is ideally suited to this kind of work. You can print a short run for family members or friends. You can choose a quality finish that reflects the care and intention behind the project. You can keep complete control over how the story is told—and who gets to read it.

This kind of publishing often has emotional weight. It can help preserve a voice that might otherwise be lost. It can bring families closer, mark a milestone, or capture a piece of social history that might not make it into the mainstream. And it often becomes a cherished object for years to come.

So if your motivation isn't financial or promotional, but personal or cultural, know that you're not alone. There's enormous value in publishing simply because the story matters.

What's Driving You?

It's worth spending a few minutes reflecting on what's really behind your decision to publish. Are you hoping for recognition? A lasting legacy? A sense of personal closure? A more profound connection with others? There's no wrong answer here—only *your* answer.

If you're clear on what's driving you, the rest of the process becomes easier. You'll know what kind of support you need, how to measure success, and where to invest your energy. That clarity is your compass.

Case Studies: The Power of Purpose

Let's look at how authors with different goals have leveraged their books:

The Consultant: A business consultant wrote a book to outline their unique methodology. The book not only attracted clients but also led to paid speaking engagements and partnerships.

The Memoirist: A cancer survivor published a memoir to inspire others going through similar challenges. Their story resonated so profoundly that it led to media interviews and an active online community.

The Entrepreneur: A bakery owner wrote a book about baking techniques, which became a bestseller on Amazon. The book boosted their brand and brought more customers to their shop.

Your purpose will shape how you write, publish, and market

your book. Defining this purpose early ensures you stay focused throughout the process.

How a Book Opens Doors

Publishing a book doesn't just benefit authors—it creates ripple effects in their personal and professional lives. Here's how:

1. Networking Opportunities

A book acts as a professional calling card. It can be handed out at conferences, events, or meetings, leaving a lasting impression. Unlike a business card, a book is rarely thrown away.

2. Credibility Boost

Being a published author sets you apart in competitive industries. It shows dedication, expertise, and the ability to produce results.

3. Legacy Creation

Books endure. Publishing allows you to leave behind something tangible—whether it's a story, insight, or knowledge—that can inspire future generations.

What Does Success Mean to You?

Success isn't always about sales. For some authors, success is holding their book in their hands. For others, it's a single heartfelt message from a reader who was moved by their story. It might be an Amazon bestseller badge, or simply completing something that once felt impossible.

Your definition of success is yours alone. Please write it down. Keep it close. It'll help you stay grounded and focused as you move through the following stages.

Brand Building

A book often acts as a cornerstone for personal branding, especially for entrepreneurs or thought leaders. It integrates seamlessly with online platforms, content strategies, and marketing efforts.

Exercise: Define Your Purpose

Take a moment to reflect on why you want to publish your book. Write down your answers to the following questions:

1. What do I want my book to achieve? (e.g., establish credibility, share a personal story, generate income).

2. Who is my target audience? (e.g., business professionals, aspiring writers, general readers).

3. How will I measure success? (e.g., sales, feedback, new opportunities).

The Common Pitfalls of Undefined Purpose

Publishing without a clear purpose can lead to frustration or unmet expectations. Here are some common mistakes to avoid:

1. Unrealistic Expectations

Expecting immediate sales or recognition without a plan can lead to disappointment. In recent years, I have been approached by authors who claim to have written the next Harry Potter, Peppa Pig, or Star Wars. Aim high, by all means, but expectations set this high are likely to lead to disappointment.

2. Audience Disconnect

Writing without a clear target audience in mind can result in a book that doesn't resonate. Always ask yourself: Who am I writing for? Be as detailed as you can. Are they male or female? How old are they? Where do they live? What do they do professionally? What are their hobbies and interests? The clearer you can be about your target reader, the more likely it is that your writing will appeal to them.

3. Misaligned Goals

A book written for the wrong reasons—such as chasing trends or following bad advice—can lack authenticity. I remember being presented with a book about how to make serious money from buying and selling houses, written by someone whose only property was the house he lived in.

Authenticity is what readers connect with most. The call for authenticity explains why AI-written books are so unlikely to succeed.

Return to Your "Why"

There will be moments when writing feels hard, when publishing feels confusing, and when the whole thing makes you wonder why you started. In those moments, go back to your original purpose. Why did you want to do this in the first place?

Your "why" isn't just your motivation—it's your anchor. It'll remind you what matters and help you keep moving forward, even when things don't go to plan.

Practical Checklist

- Clearly define your purpose for publishing.
- Identify and describe your target audience in as much detail as you can.
- Understand how your book aligns with your personal or professional goals.

Defining your purpose is the foundation of your self-publishing journey. It shapes your writing, your strategy, and your success. In the next chapter, I will outline a self-publishing model that will give your book the best possible chance of success, without breaking the bank.

4

THE THREE-STEP STRATEGY

If you've Googled "how to self-publish a book," you're probably more confused than when you started. The publishing world is full of conflicting advice, enticing promises, and companies offering to do everything for you, for a fee. Some recommend sticking solely with print-on-demand, others push you towards bulk printing, while many self-publishing companies try to lock you into their systems and formats.

And yet, so much of this advice overlooks what most self-published authors need: simplicity, control, and flexibility. That's what my recommended **three-step strategy** delivers.

This approach—used by many of my most successful author clients—combines the convenience of Amazon's print-on-demand system with the control and cost-effectiveness of bulk printing.

Create Your Publishing Map

Think of this strategy as a custom map—not a one-size-fits-all solution, but a route that lets you use the best of each publishing option without being locked in. By blending print-on-demand, eBooks and short-run printing, you stay in control while reaching different types of readers through various channels.

This isn't about choosing sides. It's about flexibility, reach, and profit. Most importantly, it's about putting you, the author, in charge.

It covers all your bases:

- Selling copies of your book throughout the world, using Amazon's (or similar) print-on-demand service.
- Having a pile of printed books, you can sell profitably at events and speaking engagements.
- Selling on Amazon as well as directly to readers via your website.
- Supplying books at trade terms to local and independent bookshops.

My **three-step strategy** ensures you have complete control over how your book is published, distributed and sold. It blends printed books and print-on-demand copies so that you can sell your book profitably to bookshops, online retailers, via your website, and face-to-face.

Let's break it down.

Step 1: Make Your Book Available (as a paperback) on Amazon via KDP

Regardless of your views on Amazon, your book needs to be available on the platform. It's the default bookstore for most readers, offering near-instant access to a global audience. Amazon's Kindle Direct Publishing (KDP) platform makes it easy to upload your book, set your price, and start selling in multiple countries—without needing to hold any stock or fulfil any orders yourself.

By listing your book with Amazon KDP, you tap into one of the most powerful book-selling machines in the world. When a customer orders your book, Amazon prints a copy and ships it directly to them, without you lifting a finger—no need for packing boxes, no postage, no stock sitting under your bed. Unless you choose to, you won't ever have to handle a single order yourself.

This system is ideal for online sales and passive income. It makes your book available 24/7, both in the UK and internationally, and allows readers to find, buy, and read your book with minimal friction.

Step 2: Make Your Book Available (as an eBook) on Amazon via KDP

With little or no additional effort, you can also publish an eBook edition of your book using the same Amazon KDP service. This will ensure that your book is accessible to Kindle readers and subscribers via Kindle Unlimited. While there are numerous other eBook retailers online, Amazon is the most significant due to the Kindle's current 74.8% market share in the e-reader market.

Beyond Kindle: Other eBook Platforms

While Amazon dominates the eBook market, it's not the only player. Platforms like Apple Books, Google Play, Kobo, and Barnes & Noble Press can help you reach new readers, especially those outside the Kindle ecosystem.

These platforms typically require separate uploads or the use of an aggregator, such as Draft2Digital or PublishDrive. You don't need to do this straight away—but it's worth knowing the options exist if you plan to grow your reach over time.

Step 3: Print Copies Separately for Your Use

Alongside your Amazon listing, you should also organise a separate print run of your book through a short-run or bulk printer. Why? Because this is how you make profitable direct sales of your book, at talks, presentations and to friends and family, as well as via your website.

This **three-step strategy** avoids two common traps that authors tend to fall into:

- They assume that if their book is published using KDP or another print-on-demand provider, they are not allowed to print copies separately using a different supplier.
- For events and speaking engagements, they purchase multiple copies of their print-on-demand edition, paying far more than necessary, which

makes it challenging to generate a significant income from direct sales.

Why Step 3 is so important

While KDP is brilliant for fulfilling Amazon orders, it doesn't make sense for direct sales. If you want to sell books at events, talks, book fairs, or to friends and family, buying your book through Amazon (even at the "author" price) often means paying more than necessary.

By printing separately, you can:

- Order high-quality books at a significantly lower cost per copy.
- Sell them directly at full price and keep 100% of the proceeds.
- Control the paper quality, cover finish, and print specs.
- Avoid the constraints of Amazon's print-on-demand setup.

This third step gives you the freedom to act as your distributor, while still benefiting from Amazon's infrastructure for online sales.

Match Your Format to Your Reader

A quick tip: choose your formats based on how your ideal reader prefers to engage with books. If your audience values signed paperbacks, ensure you've a box of books on hand. If they love audiobooks or eReaders, make digital a priority.

Format isn't just a technical choice—it's a reader experience decision.

Why the Three-Step Strategy Only Works if You Publish It Yourself

Many self-publishing companies claim to offer "support" or "partnerships," but often they prevent you from using the tools you should be using directly. If you sign up with one of these companies, you'll likely be forced to buy your book from them at an inflated print-on-demand price—even when you want to sell at an event or gift a copy to a friend. You may also find you have limited control over pricing, files, and distribution.

With my three-step strategy, you stay in charge. You set up your KDP account and manage your files. You liaise directly with your printer. You decide how, where, and for how much your book is sold. That's the power of true self-publishing—and it's why this strategy is only available to authors who choose the DIY route.

A Flexible, Future-Proof Model

What makes this strategy so powerful is its adaptability. It allows you to:

- Fulfil online orders without lifting a finger.
- Attend events with stock in hand.
- Offer signed copies directly from your website.
- Gift copies without incurring premium fees.
- Keep more of what you earn.

Whether you sell five books a month or five hundred, the three-step strategy scales with you. You can adjust your print quantities over time, experiment with new versions, or run promotions online while maintaining complete control over your offline sales.

A Quick Comparison

Amazon KDP

Upfront Costs: Low or none

Cost Per Book: Higher per unit

Stock Handling: Not required

Convenience: Fully automated

Control: Limited to Amazon's specs

Sales Opportunities: Great for online customers

Bulk Printing

Upfront Costs: Higher (but scalable)

Cost Per Book: Lower per unit (especially at volume)

Stock Handling: You handle delivery/storage

Convenience: Manual, but flexible

Control: Full control over materials and pricing

Sales Opportunities: Great for events, talks, and direct sales

. . .

The Three-Step Strategy Setup

Use this checklist to make sure you've got both parts of your strategy covered:

Step 1: Amazon KDP Setup

- Create your free KDP account at kdp.amazon.co.uk
- Format your manuscript for print (PDF) and Kindle (ePub or KPF)
- Create your own Amazon-ready cover using KDP's specifications.
- Set your retail price and territories (UK, US, global)
- Upload your book and review the test proofs if necessary.
- Publish in both paperback and Kindle formats.
- Include any reviews and a compelling author biography.

Step 2: Bulk Printing Setup

- Choose a UK-based printer (e.g., Book Printing UK, Clays, or Short Run Press)
- Request quotes for short runs (e.g., 100, 250, 500 copies)
- Confirm final trim size, paper type, and cover finish.
- Order proof copies to check quality
- Arrange safe storage (e.g., at home or via a local distributor)
- Plan where you'll sell your books (events, website, talks, shops)
- Price your copies to include a healthy margin.

Case Study: How Anna Used the Three-Step Strategy to Build Momentum

Anna is a first-time nonfiction author who wrote a practical guide for solo freelancers. She wanted her book to be available online, but she also knew she'd be speaking at business events and local networking groups where people would like to buy copies in person.

She followed the three-step strategy:

- **Step 1:** She listed her book on Amazon via KDP in both paperback and Kindle formats. This gave her global visibility and a professional online presence. She didn't have to worry about fulfilling orders, and friends abroad could easily buy her book.
- **Step 2:** She also printed 500 copies through a UK short-run printer at a cost of just under £2 per copy. At talks and workshops, she sold these for £10 each, keeping all of the £8 profit for herself. She included a sign-up slip inside the book, allowing readers to join her mailing list.

Six months later, Anna had sold 400 copies—half via Amazon and half directly. Her talks became more frequent, and she now bundles her book with her freelance coaching services. She's planning her second print run—and couldn't have done it without the flexibility the three-step strategy gave her.

The three-step strategy gives you the best of both worlds. It lets Amazon do what Amazon does best—sell books online at scale—while allowing you to take ownership of your book in the real world, with lower costs and higher returns. It's flexible, it's efficient, and it's only possible when you self-publish your book independently.

In the next chapter, we'll shift our attention to how you can prepare your manuscript for publication, ensuring it's polished, professional, and ready for the world.

5

PREPARING YOUR MANUSCRIPT

Before your book reaches readers, it needs to meet professional standards of production quality and readability, and stand proud alongside its mainstream published competition. It starts with a well-prepared manuscript, which not only reflects your commitment to quality but also determines how readers, reviewers, and industry professionals perceive your work.

This Is the Turning Point

This is where your book begins its transformation—from something private and personal to something ready for the world. It can be daunting to hand over your words to others. But it's also empowering. You're stepping into your role not just as a writer, but as a publisher—someone committed to giving readers the best experience possible.

Self-publishing offers you complete control, but with that comes the responsibility to ensure your book looks, reads, and feels professional. This chapter considers manuscript preparation, the experts you may need to involve, and how to budget effectively for these services.

Step 1: Editing

Editing is the cornerstone of a professional manuscript. It's not just about catching typos—it's about shaping your book into its best possible version. I've lost count of the number of times I have heard writers say to me things like:

"I do all my own editing!"

"My wife has read through it, and she has an English degree"

"I have shared the manuscript with friends, and they all say it's great!"

"I've accepted all Grammarly's recommendations, so the book is fully edited!"

Manuscript editing is a professional skill, and getting your manuscript professionally edited is a step you cannot overlook.

The Types of Editing

1. Developmental Editing:

This focuses on the big picture. A developmental editor helps you assess the structure of your book, identify weak spots, and refine the overall flow. For fiction, they might address pacing, character arcs, and plot inconsistencies. For nonfiction, they'll ensure clarity, logical progression, and engagement.

Example: Does your story start in the right place? Are your chapters building toward a satisfying conclusion?

I once worked with an author whose book was about technology in the workplace. It emerged that the most interesting and compelling section of the book was tucked away in an appendix. I introduced the author to a developmental editor I knew, who helped him to restructure the manuscript entirely. A few weeks later, the author got in touch to express his gratitude for the changes and how much more compelling the manuscript had become following the developmental work.

2. Line Editing:

Line editing focuses on how you tell your story. It looks at sentence structure, tone, and word choice, ensuring your writing is clear, consistent, and engaging. A line editor might suggest rephrasing awkward sentences or enhancing emotional impact.

3. Copyediting:

This is the detail-oriented stage. Copyeditors ensure that grammar, punctuation, spelling, and consistency are flawless. They also check for factual accuracy where relevant.

4. Proofreading:

The final step before publication, proofreading, catches typos, formatting inconsistencies, and any errors that slipped through earlier rounds of editing.

. . .

Why It Matters

Editing elevates your manuscript, turning good writing into excellent writing. Even bestselling authors work with editors to ensure their manuscripts are the best they can be. Readers notice quality, and a poorly edited book can result in negative reviews, which are notoriously hard to recover from.

How to Find an Editor

- Use online freelance platforms, such as Upwork.
- Use the member search facility offered by the Chartered Institute of Editing and Proofreading.
- Get recommendations from other writers and authors.
- Look in the acknowledgements of books you rate highly and see if their editor has been singled out for praise.

Before committing to an editor:

- Ask for a sample edit of a single section or chapter to ensure the editor understands your voice and goals.
- Be wary of editors who promise quick turnarounds at suspiciously low prices.
- Request references. Ask to talk to another author they have worked with.
- Ask yourself: Is this person on the same wavelength as me, and could I work with them for an extended period?

Estimated Costs

I can only offer a comprehensive guideline of editorial costs because every piece of writing is different. However, for a typical 40,000-to-60,000-word manuscript, you can expect to pay:

- Developmental Editing: £500–£2,000.
- Line/Copyediting: £500–£1,500.
- Proofreading: £300–£700.

Good editing takes time, skill, and a fundamental understanding of your voice. Choose carefully.

Step 2: Typesetting and Formatting

Once your manuscript is edited, it's ready for typesetting, which is about how the words are set out on the page. A book that reads well also needs to *look* like a proper book, inside and out.

You don't need to become a designer, but you do need to understand the basics of design. If your book doesn't look professional, it won't be taken seriously, no matter how good the writing is.

Design isn't decoration.

The purpose of design is to make your book easier and more enjoyable to read. That applies to both your cover and interior layout.

Bad design screams "amateur." Good design disappears. It allows the reader to focus on the content without being distracted by irregular line breaks, cumbersome headings, or fonts that are difficult to read.

Your goal is to produce something that feels professional, polished and effortless.

What's Involved?

Typesetting is the process of arranging your text so that it appears clean, readable, and visually balanced. It includes:

- Font choice and size
- Line spacing and margins
- Paragraph alignment and indentation
- Heading styles
- Page numbers, headers and footers

It's one of those things you only notice when it's poorly done.

Here are some basics to follow:

- Use a traditional serif font for the body text (e.g., Garamond, Minion Pro, Georgia)
- Choose a trim size that suits your book—5.5" x 8.5" is a popular UK non-fiction size.
- Keep margins wide enough that the text doesn't feel cramped.
- Justify body text, and use consistent paragraph spacing.
- Avoid widows, orphans and inconsistent line breaks.

There are tools to help. **Vellum** (Mac only) and **Atticus** (Mac/PC) are simple formatting tools designed for authors. Or you can hire a typesetter or designer via platforms like Reedsy or Fiverr.

ebooks: Formatting (rather than typesetting)

eBook formatting is more straightforward but less predictable. You don't control how your book looks on every device. Readers can change font size, style and layout at will. That's why eBook formatting is more about structure than design.

Make sure your chapters are correctly tagged. Use a clean, consistent heading structure. Avoid hard line breaks and overly complex layouts—they rarely survive the jump to Kindle or Apple Books.

If you're using Amazon KDP, upload your manuscript in a Kindle-native format (e.g. EPUB, KPF). Tools like Vellum or Scrivener make this easy.

Why It Matters

Poorly typeset and formatted text can ruin the reading experience. Pages with inconsistent margins, clunky line breaks, or fonts that are hard to read can frustrate readers and lead to negative feedback, even if the content itself is excellent.

You've probably experienced a poorly typeset book without realising it. Have you ever read a page of a book several times, without absorbing what the words were saying? Or have your eyes felt heavy and tired after reading just a page or two of a book? You probably concluded that it was just a boring book that didn't appeal to you as you hoped it would. More likely, it was down to the way the book was typeset.

How to Approach Typesetting and Formatting

- **DIY Tools:** Applications like Vellum (Mac-only) or Scrivener offer typesetting options for authors and will also convert your manuscript to a range of eBook formats.
- **Hire a Professional:** Unless you have strong design skills and a clear understanding of what you're doing, hire a professional typesetter with book trade experience.

Estimated Costs

- **Print Typesetting:** £300–£1,000.
- **eBook Formatting:** £150–£350.

Step 3: Cover Design

Your cover is the single most important visual decision you'll make. It's what readers see first—on Amazon, on social media, or at an event table.

Your cover should:

- Be genre-appropriate (a business book shouldn't look like a thriller)
- Include your title, subtitle (if you have one), and your name.
- Work in thumbnail size (especially on Amazon)

- Avoid DIY clichés (don't use Canva templates unless you know what you're doing)
- Be print-ready (including spine width and back cover text)

If you can afford it, hire a professional. A great cover designer will understand how to balance type, imagery and layout—and how to design for different formats (paperback, eBook, hardback).

Key Elements of a Great Cover

1. **Title and Subtitle:** These should be clear and readable, even at thumbnail size.
2. **Imagery:** Use visuals that resonate with your target audience. For example, a thriller might feature dark, moody imagery, while a romance novel might use softer colours and typefaces.
3. **Typography:** Fonts should complement the genre and remain easy to read. Avoid overly decorative or complex fonts.
4. **Brand Consistency:** If you plan to write a series of related books, consider how your covers will fit together as a cohesive brand.

Why It Matters

Readers *do* judge books by their covers. A professionally designed cover can make your book stand out in a crowded marketplace, while an amateurish one can discourage potential buyers.

Where to Find Designers

- **Freelancers:** Platforms like Reedsy, Fiverr, or 99designs are excellent for finding cover designers. Or visit a library and bookstore and pick out a handful of books whose covers you like in your genre. The chances are that they were designed by a freelance cover designer, who you could track down with a carefully worded Google search.
- **Premade Covers:** Some designers sell premade covers that can be customised with your title and author name.

Estimated Costs

Again, these are broad estimates for guidance only.

- **Custom Cover Design:** £250–£1,250.
- **Premade Covers:** £50–£200.

Activity: Design Audit

Take five minutes to grab a few paperbacks from your shelf —ideally books you admire or books similar to yours.

- What do you notice about the covers? The typefaces? The spacing?
- How do they handle chapter headings, margins, and page numbers?
- Do they include extras (like contents pages, pull quotes, or endnotes)?

- What design decisions help you trust the book, or put you off?

Jot down a few notes. These will help guide your own decisions as you finalise your manuscript.

Step 4: ISBN and Copyright

If you want to make your self-published book available in high-street bookshops and most online stores, it will need an ISBN (and accompanying barcode). An ISBN (International Standard Book Number) is a unique identifier for your book. It's required for listing your book with retailers, libraries, and distributors.

The method you use to obtain your ISBN will depend on how you choose to self-publish. If you opt for one of the full-service self-publishing companies, or a collaborative or hybrid publisher, they will likely supply you with the ISBN. If you choose to publish solely on Amazon, using Amazon's KDP service, then Amazon will assign a free ASIN (Amazon Standard Identification Number) as well as an ISBN.

If you follow my advice and adopt my three-step publishing strategy, you will need to purchase your own ISBN. In the UK, you can buy ISBNs from the NielsenIQ BookData ISBN Agency.

It's essential to note that if you aspire to publish more than one book, you should purchase your ISBNs, as they will then be grouped under your imprint or brand. Single ISBNs provided free of charge will usually be grouped with independently published books from a range of authors.

Copyright Protection

In most countries, including the UK, your book is automatically protected by copyright the moment it is created. No additional registration is needed, but you can add a copyright notice (e.g., © [Your Name], 2025) for clarity.

Estimated Costs

- ISBN: £89 for a single ISBN or £164 for a block of 10.
- Copyright: No additional cost (automatic protection).

Step 5: Print and paper decisions

If you're bulk printing (as part of your three-step strategy), you'll also need to make a few choices:

- **Paper weight and colour** – Most trade paperbacks use white or off-white paper, typically 80–90 gsm.
- **Cover finish** – Matte tends to feel modern and understated; gloss is bolder and more durable.
- **Binding type** – Most authors use perfect binding (like a paperback), but there are other options.

If in doubt, find a book you like the *look* of and show it to your designer or printer. It helps to have a visual reference.

How Print Quantity Affects Unit Cost

If you're thinking about printing physical copies of your book, whether via short-run digital printing or traditional litho, it pays to understand how pricing works.

Printers often use a **sliding scale:** the more copies you order, the lower the cost per book. That's because certain elements —like setting up the press, calibrating colours, or creating plates for litho—are fixed costs. Once those are covered, each additional book is relatively cheap to produce.

Here's a simplified example (these aren't real quotes, but they illustrate the idea):

Quantity	Total cost	Per copy
100 copies	£400	£4.00
250 copies	£750	£3.00
500 copies	£1,100	£2.20
1,000 copies	£1,600|	£1.60

That's why it's a good idea to ask for **multiple quotes**—typically for 100, 250, 500, and 1,000 copies. You'll often find that doubling your print run doesn't double your spend, and that small increases can lead to significant per-copy savings.

That said, don't let the lower unit cost seduce you into ordering more books than you can realistically sell or store. Printing 1,000 books at £1.60 each is only cost-effective if you're confident you can shift them. Otherwise, you'll end up with boxes of books and no room in your airing cupboard.

Tip: When requesting quotes, always ask for both digital and litho options (if you're printing more than 750–1,000 copies). Digital printing is cost-effective for shorter runs, but litho becomes more efficient at scale, particularly for black-and-white interiors or high-page-count books.

Working with a Printer

If you choose to print copies in bulk — whether 50 or 500 — it's worth understanding how your printer works behind the scenes. Most short-run printers (like Short Run Press here in the UK) will guide you through each step, but knowing the basics makes the process smoother and helps you avoid unnecessary delays or surprises.

Here are a few practical tips:

• **Plan your cover properly:**

Your printer will calculate your book's spine width based on your page count and paper type. Always confirm this before sending final files. Covers should be supplied as a full spread (back, spine, front) with a standard 3mm bleed for paperbacks.

• **Use sections wisely:**

Printers bind pages in sections, typically in blocks of 16 or 32 pages. Keeping your total page count to an even multiple helps avoid blank pages or extra costs. If you want to insert a glossy photo section, leave those pages unnumbered so it can drop in cleanly.

• **Mind the margins:**

Content that spans two pages (such as wide tables or large images) can be obscured by the spine. Keep vital text and artwork clear of the gutter — or speak to your printer's pre-press team for advice.

. . .

• **Understand proofs:**

Most printers will provide a PDF proof, allowing you to review the layout and page order. Some offer printed proofs if your book relies on precise colour. Allow extra time (and budget) if you want this step.

• **Talk about finishes:**

If you would like special touches, such as foil blocking, Spot UV, or cloth binding, please request them early. Your printer may need custom files (usually black-only artwork for foiling or varnish) and extra production time.

• **Delivery and storage:**

Boxes of books are heavy! Know where you'll store them, how you'll pack them for postage, and whether you want multiple delivery addresses. Most printers can assist you in planning this.

Working directly with a printer gives you more control over quality and cost, and often results in better unit prices once you reach 100 or more copies. The key is clear communication: ask questions, follow their file specs, and don't be afraid to lean on their expertise.

Case Studies: Preparing for Success

1. The Meticulous Writer

Nonfiction author Colin hired both a developmental editor and a proofreader to ensure their book was both insightful and error-free. The extra investment paid off in glowing reviews and strong word-of-mouth recommendations.

2. The Designer on a Budget

Romance novelist Judy used a premade cover from a trusted designer and focused their budget on quality typesetting. The result was a professional-looking book that resonated with readers.

3. The First-Time Author

Debut author Liz chose to learn eBook formatting through Vellum, allowing her to save on costs while still achieving a polished result. She invested the savings in marketing her book after its launch.

Activity: Create Your Checklist

Service	Provider/Source	Estimated Cost (£)	Notes
Editing			
Typesetting (for print)			
eBook Formatting			
Cover Design			
Print			
ISBN			

Professionalism Is a Form of Respect

Producing a well-edited, professionally presented book isn't about vanity. It's about respect—respect for your reader, for your ideas, and for the journey you've been on to get this far.

When your book reads smoothly, looks polished, and is free from careless errors, readers are more likely to trust you and recommend your work to others. In a crowded marketplace, that matters.

Preparing your manuscript is the most critical step in self-publishing. High-quality editing, typesetting, eBook formatting and design ensure that your book is not only readable but competitive in today's crowded market.

In the next chapter, we'll explore whether some of the publishing technology and AI applications that have emerged in recent years can streamline your publishing journey and enhance the results you achieve.

6

LEVERAGING TECHNOLOGY AND AI

Self-publishing in 2025 can feel incredibly exciting, thanks in large part to advances in technology and artificial intelligence (AI). From drafting and amending to marketing and sales, tools have emerged that make it easier—and often faster—to publish a professional-quality book. However, while technology is a powerful ally, it's not a replacement for your creativity or the human touch.

This chapter explores the technology that exists, and how to use it without compromising your book's creativity, integrity or originality.

What Technology and AI Can Do

The right tools can save time, improve productivity, consistency and potentially the quality of your work. Here's how technology can assist in key areas:

· · ·

1. Writing and Drafting

AI-powered tools like ChatGPT, Jasper AI, and Sudowrite can help you brainstorm ideas, overcome writer's block, and even draft sections of your book. These tools excel at generating content quickly, summarising and paraphrasing, and explaining complex concepts in simple terms.

As a writer, you need to understand what these tools can and can't do and use them only when they improve your work. Ask them to generate a list of topics, by all means. Perhaps even ask for an outline of each one. But then write about each topic yourself. AI-generated writing can sound robotic, and by definition, won't have your voice, creativity, or expertise.

- *Example*: Struggling with a chapter introduction? Provide the AI with a prompt, and it can suggest multiple starting points.
- *Caution*: While AI can assist with drafting, the core ideas and voice should always come from you.

Technology as Your Co-Pilot

Think of technology as your co-pilot, not the pilot taking control of the plane. You're still "flying" the book. You set the direction, pace, and destination. Tools like ChatGPT or Grammarly can help you navigate, spot hazards, and suggest shortcuts. But you're the one in the seat.

This mindset keeps you in charge and reminds you that tools should support your creativity, not replace it.

2. Editing and Proofreading

Technology like Grammarly offers a degree of editing support and will analyse your writing for grammar, spelling, tone, and even readability. These tools are excellent for catching errors and refining your prose before sending it to a professional editor.

However, I have worked with authors who rely too heavily on tools like Grammarly. They routinely review and accept every suggestion Grammarly has made, whether they agree with it or not. This is not the intended use of tools like this, and you should follow their recommendations as a guide rather than a strict instruction.

- *Strengths*: Instant feedback, suggestions for concise writing, and consistency checks.
- *Limitations*: These tools lack the nuance of a human editor and may miss contextual issues.

3. Typesetting and Formatting

Tools like Vellum and Atticus simplify the process of organising, typesetting and formatting your book for print and digital platforms. They allow you to create professional layouts without needing to hire design expertise.

If your book is mainly text, and you favour a straightforward page layout, then I encourage you to give them a try. In addition to laying out pages, they are also helpful in managing your various completed and unfinished chapters, sections, and ideas that make up the book.

- *Benefits*: User-friendly interfaces, customisable templates, and compatibility with major platforms like Amazon KDP and Apple Books.
- *Drawbacks*: Limited to standard layouts—custom designs still require professional help.

4. Cover Design

AI-powered design tools, such as Canva and Adobe Express, can help you create polished book covers without needing to hire a designer. These tools offer templates and drag-and-drop functionality, making it easier to experiment with layouts, fonts, and images. Increasingly, they incorporate AI to create designs based on descriptive prompts from you.

In my experience, however, these tools promise more than they deliver. You get the best results from them if you already have a natural aptitude for design. If, like me, you have very few design skills, then tools like Canva won't suddenly turn you into a professional cover designer. So I always leave something as crucial as a cover design to a professional.

- *When to Use*: For premade or placeholder covers during the drafting process.
- *When Not to Use*: For final publication, professional design consistently outperforms DIY efforts, unless you have design experience yourself.

5. Marketing and Promotion

AI and tech tools can also support your marketing efforts. Examples include:

- **Hootsuite/Buffer:** Schedule and automate social media posts.
- **Mailchimp:** Build and manage email campaigns to promote your book.
- **AI Analytics:** Tools like Google Analytics help track website traffic and audience engagement.
- **AI to Enhance Your Visibility:** AI tools can also help increase the visibility of your book. Try asking for keyword suggestions for your book's Amazon listing or blog posts. Use those keywords to shape your subtitle, description, or promotional copy. This doesn't replace human marketing strategy, but it can help you make smarter, more informed decisions about how your book shows up online.

Since the beginning of 2025, I have been experimenting with several AI tools to assess how they can support my writing, as well as the marketing and promotion of my books. Although many studies resulted in disappointment, several others delivered outstanding results, including:

1. Suggesting a series of social media posts and articles (tailored for each platform) to engage with readers of my latest book.
2. Researching clubs, societies and forums online

where I could find and engage with potential readers in my genre.

3. Writing copy for my Amazon book listing, as well as for the back cover of the book itself.

4. Putting together a list of independent bookshops by the sea, and close to a prominent lighthouse (it's a long story!).

With results like these, I encourage you to learn more about how AI tools like ChatGPT, Gemini, and Co-Pilot work and to experiment with ways they might support you.

Staying Organised and Backed Up

Beyond writing and marketing, technology can also help you stay on top of the many moving parts of self-publishing. Tools like Trello, Notion or Google Sheets can help you track deadlines, assign tasks, and manage collaborators.

And don't forget file backup—seriously. Use Dropbox, Google Drive or iCloud to keep your manuscript safe and accessible from anywhere. Losing a file is frustrating; losing a nearly finished book is something else entirely.

What Technology and AI Shouldn't Do

While technology is powerful, it has limitations. Here are tasks you should avoid outsourcing entirely to AI:

1. Crafting Your Book's Voice

AI tools are excellent for generating ideas, but they lack your unique perspective, creativity, and authenticity. Your voice is what makes your book stand out.

2. Final Proofreading

While tools like Grammarly catch many errors, they can miss contextual or stylistic nuances. A professional proof-reader or editor is essential for the final review.

3. Marketing Strategy

AI can analyse trends and provide suggestions, but the overarching strategy and messaging should come from you or a professional marketer who understands your audience.

Tools for Authors: A Guide

Here's a curated list of tools you can use at various stages of your self-publishing journey:

Stage	Tool	Purpose
Writing and Drafting	ChatGPT, Gemini	Brainstorming ideas, generating content drafts.
Editing	Grammarly, ProWritingAid	Grammar, tone, and style refinement.
Formatting	Vellum, Atticus	Creating print and eBook layouts.
Cover Design	Canva, Adobe Express	Designing placeholder or draft covers.
Marketing	Mailchimp, Hootsuite	Email campaigns and social media automation.

AI Isn't Just for Authors — Publishers Use It Too

The AI landscape is changing quickly, so keep an eye out for new tools and consider how each one might support your writing. Never hand over your writing entirely to AI — but do recognise that these tools can help you work smarter. In fact, some publishers now use the same technology that savvy authors rely on to strengthen their own editorial process.

A good example is Bloodhound Books, who recently partnered with ProWritingAid to help assess and tighten the editorial structure of the books they publish. So if a mainstream publisher trusts and uses an AI-powered tool to ensure your writing meets a certain standard, it makes perfect sense for you to do the same.

Think of it not as cutting corners, but as raising your manuscript's game. Use tools like ProWritingAid to check consistency, flow and clarity — so your human editor can spend their time polishing the big-picture details that software can't handle.

Case Studies: Enhancing with AI

1. The Time-Strapped Writer

A copywriting friend, Josh, used ChatGPT to brainstorm ideas for blog posts that later became chapters in his nonfiction book. It helped him organise ideas quickly, saving hours in the drafting process.

2. The Marketing-Savvy Author

Sue is a local author of novels about smugglers. She used Canva to create Instagram graphics promoting her books. She scheduled her social media posts with Buffer, ensuring consistent engagement with readers.

3. The Independent DIYer

I encouraged my friend Hannah to try out Vellum to typeset her manuscript for print and format it for publication as an eBook. The finished result was a decent-looking, polished product that she accomplished without hiring a typesetter.

Activity: Experiment with AI

Take 30 minutes to explore how AI can support your self-publishing process. Try one of the following exercises:

1. Use ChatGPT or Jasper AI to generate a sample introduction for your book.
2. Upload a chapter into Grammarly or ProWritingAid and review the suggested edits.
3. Design a mock book cover using Canva or Adobe Express.

Reflect on what worked, what didn't, and how you might use these tools in the future.

Practical Checklist

- Identify the technology and AI tools that best fit your self-publishing needs.
- Understand the strengths and limitations of each tool.
- Experiment with at least one tool to streamline your process.

Technology and AI are transforming the way authors write, publish, and market their books. These tools offer tremendous opportunities to save time, increase productivity, and reach readers more effectively. However, success still hinges on your creativity, vision, and effort.

In the next chapter, we'll explore ghostwriting and collaborative writing.

7

GHOSTWRITING AND COLLABORATIVE WRITING

If you've got a book idea but struggle to find the time or confidence to write it yourself, you may be tempted by the promise of ghostwriters, book coaches, or collaborative publishing teams who'll "write it with you" or "turn your ideas into a book."

This support can be genuinely helpful, but it can also be expensive. This chapter will help you understand what's possible, what's risky, and how to stay in control of your book, whether you write every word or not.

What is ghostwriting?

A ghostwriter is someone you hire to write a book for you, usually based on interviews, notes, recordings, or a detailed brief. Their job is to capture your voice, your story, or your expertise, and turn it into a publishable manuscript. In most cases, the ghostwriter is paid a flat fee and doesn't get a cover credit.

Some well-known authors use ghostwriters. So do business leaders, celebrities, and busy professionals with compelling stories but limited time.

Collaborative writing and book coaching

Some service companies offer something slightly different: "collaborative" writing or coaching. Here, you're more involved in shaping the book. You might supply the content (as raw writing, blog posts, audio notes), and the writer helps you structure, refine or rewrite it. Others provide coaching sessions to help you clarify your ideas and keep the project moving.

This can work well *if* the writer is experienced, honest, and the price is fair.

When might you consider it?

You might want to explore a ghostwriter or collaborator if:

- You know what you want to say, but struggle with written communication.
- You need a fast turnaround for business or PR reasons.
- You're better at speaking than writing, and want someone to shape your transcripts.
- You're writing a memoir or life story, but find the emotional process challenging to navigate on your own.

Be Clear About Roles and Rights

If you bring someone in to help, it's essential to agree—up front—on who's doing what. Will they write from scratch or work with your material? Will you give feedback chapter-by-chapter, or just at the end?

Agree on payment terms, timelines, and ownership of assets. If there's any chance of shared royalties, make sure it's in writing. Clarity now saves conflict later.

Warning signs to watch for

Unfortunately, this space is full of opportunists. Be wary of anyone who:

- Quotes £20,000+ without clear deliverables
- Bundles in vague "publishing support" without detail
- Won't let you own the rights or source files
- Promises bestseller status or guaranteed income
- Pushes you to commit on the first call

Always ask:

- Who will be writing the book?
- Can I see samples of their work?
- What happens if I'm not happy with the writing?
- Will I retain all rights to the manuscript?

How to Vet a Ghostwriter or Collaborator

- Ask to see previous work—preferably similar to your book's genre or tone.
- Request client testimonials or references.
- Talk to them. Are they easy to communicate with? Do they "get" your book?
- Check: Are they asking you thoughtful questions, or just pitching to you?

Choose someone you'd be happy to spend hours working with. Because you probably will.

Alternatives to full ghostwriting

If you don't want to write the whole thing yourself, but still want it to be *your* book, consider:

- **A writing coach** – Someone to guide and support you, without doing it for you.
- **A developmental editor** – Someone who helps you shape your ideas and structure, once you've made a start.
- **Speech-to-text tools** – Record yourself talking through your ideas, then edit the transcripts.

These approaches provide support, without relinquishing control or ownership.

Don't Lose Your Voice

Even if someone else is helping you write, your book still needs to sound like *you*. Make sure they've read your other work, listened to you speak, or seen examples of your writing style. Be clear about tone, phrasing, and anything that matters to you.

And always ask for drafts along the way. That way, you can tweak and steer before things go too far off track.

Author Solutions vs. Vanity Presses

Not all paid publishing services are created equal.

Some companies describe themselves as offering "assisted publishing," "hybrid publishing," or "author solutions." These can range from legitimate, helpful providers to over-priced, underperforming vanity presses.

Here's how to spot the difference:

✅ Legitimate Partner	✖ Vanity Press
Transparent pricing	Hidden costs or inflated packages
You retain full rights	They ask for rights or control of ISBNs
Selective about projects	Say yes to everything
Offers real editorial/design expertise	Pushes expensive upsells with vague benefits
You choose how profits are handled	They keep a cut or take full royalties
You're free to print/distribute elsewhere	You're locked into their platform or system

A good assisted publishing partner will behave more like a project manager or consultant, supporting you rather than trapping you.

If the company promises success, charts, or awards... walk away. No one can guarantee that.

. . .

Always ask:

- Who owns the rights?
- Where will the book be sold?
- Can I print it elsewhere?
- What am I paying for?

Activity: What kind of support do you need?

Answer these questions honestly:

- What's stopping me from writing this book on my own?
- Do I lack time, skill, motivation, or something else?
- Do I want someone to write *for* me, or help me write better?
- What part of the process do I need most help with —planning, writing, editing, or accountability?

Your answers will help you find the right kind of support, if any, and avoid paying for services you don't need.

In the next chapter, we'll explore your author brand and explain why it is essential.

8

BUILDING YOUR AUTHOR BRAND

Publishing a book is more than just sharing your words with the world—it's also an opportunity to create a lasting impression as an author. Your *brand* is the way readers perceive you and your work. A strong author brand establishes trust, fosters loyalty, and lays the groundwork for a lasting relationship with your readers. Whether you plan to publish one book or many, developing a recognisable and consistent brand will help you connect with your audience and set yourself apart in a crowded market.

In this chapter, we explore how to define your brand, establish your presence, and communicate effectively with your readers.

Defining Your Brand

"Brand" is an off-putting word for many writers, but all it means is *what people remember about you*. Your author brand is made up of:

- How you write.
- How you present yourself.
- How you communicate.
- How people think of you.

If your writing is warm and funny, but your website is stiff and formal, something will feel off. If your cover is professional, but your bio is full of in-jokes, readers may get confused.

You don't need a logo or tagline. However, you do need a consistent tone and a clear sense of how you want to present yourself.

Your author brand is the essence of who you are as a writer and what you offer your readers. It's not just about your books—it's about the emotions, themes, and experiences your work delivers. To define your brand, start by reflecting on what makes you unique. Consider the themes you explore in your writing. Are your stories filled with heart-warming moments, spine-tingling twists, or practical advice that changes lives? Think about your ideal reader. Who are they, and what are they seeking from your books? What impression do you want to leave? Do you want to be seen as an expert, a storyteller, or a source of inspiration?

For example, if you write romance novels, your brand might emphasise warmth, escapism, and happily-ever-afters. On the other hand, a business author might focus on expertise, innovation, and actionable strategies. Understanding your brand at this foundational level will inform every decision you make, from your cover designs to the way you interact with your audience.

Your Brand Is a Promise

Your author brand isn't just a style or colour scheme—it's a promise. When someone picks up your book or visits your website, they're expecting a particular kind of experience. That might be a warm and funny escape, a sharp hit of expert insight, or a moment of deep reflection.

Whatever your promise is, ensure that you consistently deliver it across your writing, design, and communications.

Show, Don't Tell

The best brands don't just *say* what they stand for—they *show* it. If you care about kindness, make that part of how you interact online. If your writing is bold and challenging, let your design and messaging reflect that same boldness and challenge. Actions speak louder than taglines. Let readers *feel* what you're about, without needing to be told.

Case Studies: What an Author's Brand Can Deliver

1. The M&A Expert

Business Book author Jonathan's brand is based on his practical, no-nonsense approach and his expertise in business acquisitions. His brand values highlight his integrity and authenticity, which have gained him a reputation as the UK's leading authority on mergers and acquisitions.

2. The Parenting Support You Never Knew You Needed

Parenting expert Sue's author brand is all about approachability and expertise. She is the calm voice ready to step in and support anxious parents. She's kind-natured, approachable, and enormous fun to spend time with. Her many books on parenting have led Sue to daytime television, where she has become a regular fixture as a parenting expert.

Creating a Consistent Presence

Consistency is the cornerstone of a strong author brand. Readers should be able to recognise your work and associate it with a particular style or experience. This consistency extends beyond your books to your online presence, marketing materials, and interactions with your audience.

Start by establishing your 'visual' identity. Choose colours, fonts, and imagery that reflect the tone and themes of your writing. For instance, a thriller author might use dark tones and bold typography, while a children's author could opt for bright colours and playful designs. Apply this visual identity across your book covers, website, and social media profiles to create a unified look.

Your voice and tone should also remain consistent. Whether you're writing a blog post, sharing a tweet, or sending a newsletter, your communication should align with your brand. A light-hearted fiction writer might use a conversational tone, while a nonfiction author might adopt a more authoritative style.

Consistency in engagement is equally important. Interact with your readers regularly and authentically. Respond to comments, share behind-the-scenes glimpses into your writing process, and celebrate milestones with your audience. Building a personal connection helps readers feel invested in your journey and eager to support your work.

What should your author biography say?

Your author biography is often the second thing a reader looks at, after your title and blurb. It's where they decide if you're the sort of person they want to read.

The most effective biographies strike a balance between credibility and personality. They're short, clear, and tailored to the reader, not the writer's ego.

A good biography usually includes:

- Who are you (briefly)?
- What qualifies you to write this book?
- A few warm, humanising details.
- An optional line about your other work.
- Where to find out more.

Keep it under 100 words, unless you're writing it for a website or speaker event.

Tips for writing your author biography

- **Write in the third person:** This is standard for most author biographies, and it keeps things neat.
- **Don't list every qualification;** include only those that are relevant. This isn't LinkedIn.

- **Be human:** A small personal detail—where you live, what you love—goes a long way.
- **Avoid over-promising:** You don't need to say you're a thought leader. Let the book speak for itself.
- **Use your natural voice:** If you wouldn't say it in conversation, don't write it in your bio.

Example Biographies

Example 1 – Non-fiction (Business book)

Anna James is a leadership coach who specialises in helping creative teams thrive. She has worked with start-ups, charities, and national organisations for over 15 years. This is her first book. Anna lives in Brighton and drinks far too much coffee.

Example 2 – Memoir

Tom Malik grew up in Manchester and now lives on the south coast. After retiring from a career in the NHS, he wrote this book to share a story that had stayed with him for decades. He's still not sure whether it's a happy ending.

Example 3 – Personal development

Rachel Moore is a former teacher and home education consultant. She has worked with hundreds of families as they navigate the transition to learning outside the classroom. This is the second book in her 'Learning at Home' series. When she's not writing, she's probably gardening.

Your Author Photo

You don't *need* one, but it can be helpful. Readers like to know who's talking to them.

If you can afford a professional headshot, great. If not, choose a clear, relaxed photo that feels like *you*, ideally with good lighting and no distractions in the background.

Avoid:

- Blurry selfies.
- Cropped family holiday snaps.
- Overly serious or moody poses (unless that matches your book).

Use Your Blog to Reinforce Your Brand

Your blog isn't just a place to share tips or updates—it's one of the best tools you have to show people who you are. Write posts that reflect your values, your voice, and your area of expertise. Over time, your blog becomes an archive of trust: a place readers can get to know you, and a reason for them to keep coming back.

Where Your Biography Will Appear

Make sure you adapt your biography slightly depending on where it's going:

- **Back cover:** Keep it to 1–2 lines, max.
- **Amazon Author Central:** A slightly longer, friendly tone is recommended, allowing for the inclusion of links.

- **Inside the book:** Include your short biography alongside a photo and website link.
- **Press releases/talks:** Adapt it to match the context (and audience).

Activity: Write Your Author Bio

Answer these prompts:

1. What's your name, and what do you do (in the context of this book)?
2. What qualifies you to write about this topic, or what experience led to the book?
3. What's one personal detail or value you want to include?
4. Where can people find out more about you or your work?

Now turn those into a 3–4 sentence biography, written in the third person. Keep it relaxed but clear.

Practical Tools for Branding

Fortunately, there are many tools available to help you establish and maintain your author brand. Canva, for instance, is an excellent platform for designing professional graphics and branding materials, even if you have little design experience. Websites like Wix and Squarespace offer easy-to-use templates for creating a polished author website that showcases your books and personality. Social media platforms like Instagram, Facebook, and Twitter (formerly known as X) offer opportunities to engage directly with readers, share updates, and cultivate a loyal community.

Each of these tools can enhance your branding efforts, but remember, the heart of your brand is *you*. Authenticity is what resonates most with readers, so let your personality and passion shine through every interaction.

Building your author brand is about more than creating a professional image—it's about forming genuine connections with your readers. By defining what makes you *you*, maintaining consistency across platforms, and using practical tools like Canva, you can create a brand that resonates and inspires loyalty. With a strong brand in place, you're not just publishing a book; you are building a lasting legacy.

In the next chapter, we'll explore how to market and promote your book effectively, ensuring it finds its audience.

9

MASTERING BOOK MARKETING AND PROMOTION

Writing and publishing your book is a significant achievement—but if you stop there, you risk your book never being seen, read, or bought. Publishing a book doesn't make it sell. Marketing does.

That may feel daunting, especially if you're not naturally comfortable with self-promotion. But here's the good news: book marketing isn't about shouting the loudest. It's about finding your readers and showing them why your book is worth their time.

And it starts *before* your book is published.

This chapter is a practical introduction to book marketing for self-published authors. We'll explore how to build your audience, create your promotional plan, use online tools effectively, and give your book the best possible chance of success.

. . .

Marketing Starts With Observation

Before you start promoting your book, start by watching. Who's your reader? What do they enjoy, and where do they spend their time online? What kinds of covers catch their eye? What questions are they asking in reviews or forums?

Good marketing doesn't begin with noise—it starts with noticing. The more you understand your readers, the easier it becomes to talk to them in a way that feels natural.

Step 1: Start With the End in Mind

Ask yourself: *Who is this book for?* Be specific. Your book isn't for "everyone"—it's for a particular type of reader. Define them clearly:

- What are they interested in?
- What other books do they read?
- Where do they spend time online?
- What problems do they have—or stories they're drawn to?

Understanding this will guide all your subsequent actions.

Once you know who you're talking to, ask: *What do I want this book to achieve?* Is it to sell a certain number of copies? Build your mailing list? Attract clients? Start conversations? Your goal shapes your strategy.

Build a Clear Reader Profile

Try to picture a specific person reading your book. What else do they read? Do they scroll Instagram for parenting tips, or browse business books on LinkedIn? Are they Kindle-only, or do they still browse the shelves in Waterstones on Saturdays?

This mental picture isn't just for fun—it guides everything from your blurb to your blog content to the way you price and promote the book. The clearer your reader profile, the more strategic you can be.

Step 2: Craft Your Message

You need a short, clear message that explains what your book is, who it's for, and why they should care. Think of this as your elevator pitch. It should answer:

- What is the book about?
- Why is it relevant or useful?
- What's unique about it?

You'll use this pitch everywhere—on your website, Amazon page, podcast interviews, and social media bios. It should feel natural, not salesy.

Step 3: Build Your Author Platform

Your *author platform* is the combination of all the places where you and your book can be discovered. You don't need to be on every platform, but you do need some way for readers to find and connect with you.

Website and Blog

- A simple website with a homepage, about page, and book info is plenty to start.

- Include an email sign-up form.
- Use a blog to share helpful or interesting content related to your book.

Email List

This is the single most valuable marketing tool you have.

- Start collecting email addresses *before* the book comes out.
- Offer a free lead magnet—like a sample chapter, checklist, or short ebook.
- Send regular, friendly updates. Be helpful, not spammy.

Amazon Author Central

Claim your Amazon author page and add a photo, bio, and links. This builds trust and boosts visibility.

Step 4: Use Social Media Strategically

Social media can be powerful, but it works best when you focus on building connections, rather than constantly promoting yourself. Select one or two platforms where your readers typically spend their time.

Instagram and TikTok

- Great for visual content, quotes, and behind-the-scenes posts.
- Use hashtags relevant to your genre or topic.

- Consider creating short videos, such as book teasers, tips, or personal reflections, to engage your audience.

Facebook

- Suitable for groups and communities.
- Set up an author page.
- Join or create a group for your niche or genre.

LinkedIn

- Ideal for non-fiction, business or self-help books.
- Publish helpful posts, connect with professionals, and build your authority.

Twitter/X

- Useful for sharing news, quotes, links and joining writing conversations.
- Use lists to follow readers, reviewers, journalists, and authors.

Be yourself. Be useful. Don't overcommit—consistency matters more than frequency.

Step 5: Generate Pre-Launch Buzz

Your book launch isn't a single day—it's a season. Build anticipation in the weeks leading up to publication.

. . .

Pre-launch tactics:

- Share the cover reveal.
- Post sample pages or quotes.
- Run a countdown.
- Invite advanced readers (ARC readers) and ask for early reviews.
- Offer a pre-order discount or bonus.
- Schedule interviews, podcast appearances, or blog guest posts.

Don't just say, "My book is out." Give people a reason to care.

Step 6: Leverage Reviews and Endorsements

Positive reviews drive sales. Ask early readers to leave honest reviews on Amazon and Goodreads. Never pay for fake reviews—it damages your credibility.

- Make it easy: send direct links to your book's review page.
- Encourage short reviews—1–2 sentences is enough.
- Share reviews on your website and social media.

Endorsements from respected names in your field can add credibility. Reach out politely, share a summary, and explain why their endorsement would be meaningful to your readers.

Step 7: Use Advertising Wisely

Paid ads can boost visibility, but they must be used carefully.

Amazon Ads

- Appear on search results and book pages.
- Target readers of similar books.
- Start with small budgets and test different keywords.

Facebook and Instagram Ads

- Highly targeted based on interests and demographics.
- Works well for niche non-fiction.
- Craft concise, benefits-driven copy and visually compelling content.

Book promotion sites

- Sites like BookBub, Freebooksy and Bargain Booksy can promote discounted ebooks to large audiences.
- These are more effective for series or building momentum over time.

Monitor your return on investment. Ads are a tool, not a magic bullet.

Step 8: Appear in Other People's Spaces

Collaborations can dramatically expand your reach. Try:

- **Podcasts:** Pitch yourself as a guest with a helpful angle.

- **Guest blogs:** Write articles that offer value to someone else's audience.
- **Influencers:** Reach out to bookstagrammers, bloggers or YouTubers in your niche.
- **Events:** Speak at meetups, book festivals, or online webinars.

The more you show up in helpful, relevant ways, the more visible you become.

Step 9: Keep Momentum Going

The work doesn't end when the book is published. Set a 3–6 month marketing plan that includes:

- Regular posts or newsletters.
- Ongoing email list building.
- Periodic promotions or discounts.
- Opportunities to re-engage readers (e.g. bonus content or follow-up Q&A).

If you're writing more books, link them together and build your platform with each one.

Activity: Build Your Marketing Plan

Answer these questions to build a basic marketing plan:

1. Who is my target reader?
2. What's my core message or pitch?
3. What platforms will I focus on?
4. What will I offer to grow my mailing list?
5. What content can I create before launch?

6. What's my launch week plan?
7. What will I do in the three months after launch?

Create a simple calendar—then stick to it.

Marketing Is a Long Game

Book marketing isn't a one-week push. It's a long game—a steady rhythm of showing up, sharing useful or entertaining content, and building trust with your audience.

You don't need to be everywhere. You don't need to post every day. But you *do* need to keep going—especially when it feels like no one's watching yet. That's how audiences grow: slowly, quietly, and then all at once.

Final Thoughts

Marketing doesn't mean becoming someone you're not. It means finding readers who'll value your work—and helping them discover it. Yes, it takes time and effort. But it's worth it.

The most successful self-published authors don't just write great books. They give those books the chance to be seen, shared and sold.

In the next chapter, we'll explore blogging and building an online presence.

10

BLOGGING AND BUILDING AN ONLINE PRESENCE

You don't need to be a full-time blogger to benefit from a blog. Most self-published authors shouldn't be. But if you're serious about building long-term visibility for your book, having some online presence—especially a blog or content hub—can make a real difference.

This chapter is about using blogging strategically: to build trust, attract readers, and support your book without it taking over your life.

Why bother with blogging?

A well-written blog helps you:

- Show up in search results (especially if your topic is niche or practical).
- Build trust with potential readers before they buy.
- Create content that you can reuse elsewhere (emails, social media, press outreach).

- Give people a reason to visit your website and join your mailing list.

It's also one of the few promotional tools capable of delivering long-term results. A good blog post can keep attracting new visitors for months—or even years—after it's published.

You don't need to post every week.

Consistency matters more than volume. You're not trying to become a content factory. Aim for 6–10 useful posts that are genuinely helpful to your target readers.

Each post should:

- Be helpful, entertaining or insightful.
- Reflect your tone and values.
- Be written in plain English.
- Include a call to action (like signing up for your mailing list, or buying your book).

Think of your blog as an extension of your book's purpose, not a dumping ground for thoughts.

Make Your Blog Search-Friendly

If you want people to find your blog through Google, a few simple steps can help:

- Use clear, descriptive titles (e.g., "How to Publish a Non-fiction Book" rather than "My Thoughts on Publishing").
- Add keywords your audience might search for.

- Write a short meta description (1–2 sentences summarising the post).
- Use headings and relevant image names.

You don't need to become an SEO expert—keep it reader-friendly and purposeful.

Plan with a Content Calendar

A simple content calendar—just a spreadsheet or notebook —can help you stay on track. Brainstorm a list of topics, jot down rough headlines, and schedule posts in advance where possible. That way, you're not scrambling for ideas or writing in a panic.

Planning also helps you spot gaps, build consistency, and align your posts with your book's themes or launch dates.

What should you blog about?

Start with topics that:

- Tie in with your book's content or themes.
- Answer common questions from your readers.
- Share your story or process.
- Offer tips or advice related to your expertise.
- Link to upcoming events, launches or interviews.

Examples:

- "5 things I learned while writing my book on X".
- "How I published my book without using a publishing company".

- "The one chapter that almost didn't make it into the final book".
- "If you liked my book, here's what to read next".

Blog vs social media

Social media moves fast. Posts vanish within hours, and you don't own the platform. Your blog, on the other hand, is yours. It's a permanent, searchable archive—and it doesn't rely on an algorithm to be found.

Use social media to share and amplify your blog posts, not as a replacement for them.

How to get started

1. Add a blog section to your website (most web builders include this by default).
2. Pick a handful of topics you feel confident writing about.
3. Draft your first post using clear, natural language— don't try to sound clever.
4. Add a clear next step for the reader (e.g., "Want more like this? Join my list").
5. Share your post via email or social media.

If you're stuck, think: *what would be genuinely helpful to someone interested in my book?*

Choosing Where to Blog

Most website platforms—like Squarespace, Wix, or Word-Press—include a blog feature by default. If you're starting from scratch, WordPress gives you a lot of control over how your blog looks and functions. Medium is another option—it's free, easy to use, and has a built-in audience. That said, you don't *own* the platform in the same way.

Wherever you blog, make sure the setup feels sustainable and straightforward. You want a space that makes writing and sharing easy, not one that becomes a technical headache.

Activity: Brainstorm 5 Blog Post Ideas

Try starting with one of each:

- A story from your writing or publishing journey.
- A practical how-to or top tips post.
- A behind-the-scenes look at your research or inspiration.
- A post answering a question your readers often ask.
- A list of resources or tools related to your book topic.

Once you've written one post, add it to your site and link to it in your email footer, bio, or Amazon author page.

In the next chapter, we will consider the various options for distributing your self-published book.

11

UNDERSTANDING DISTRIBUTION CHANNELS

Distribution is the bridge between your book and your readers. It's the process of making your book available in places where people can buy or access it, whether that's online, in bookstores, or through libraries. As a self-published author, you have the power to choose how and where your book is distributed. However, with numerous options available, it's essential to understand their advantages, limitations, and how they align with your publishing objectives.

In this chapter, we will explore the key distribution channels available to self-published authors, consider the benefits and challenges of each, and provide guidance on how to navigate this critical part of the publishing process.

Exclusive vs. Wide Distribution

One of the first decisions to make concerns your eBook, and

whether to distribute it exclusively on a single platform or make it widely available across multiple channels.

Exclusive Distribution

Exclusive distribution means publishing your book through a single platform, such as Amazon KDP, and opting into programs like Kindle Unlimited (KU). KU allows subscribers to read your eBook for free while you earn royalties based on the number of pages read. This approach simplifies distribution and provides you with access to Amazon's powerful promotional tools, including countdown deals and free book promotions.

However, exclusive distribution comes with limitations. By choosing this path, you agree not to sell your eBook on other platforms, which restricts your ability to reach readers who prefer alternatives like Apple Books or Kobo.

Wide Distribution

Wide distribution involves making your book available on multiple platforms, such as Amazon, Apple Books, Google Play, and Kobo. It also allows you to distribute print copies through channels like IngramSpark, which makes your book accessible to bookstores and libraries worldwide.

While a wide distribution broadens your reach, it requires more effort to manage, as each platform has its own requirements and promotional opportunities. It also means forfeiting some of the exclusive benefits Amazon offers.

Don't Forget the Aggregators

Managing your book across lots of platforms can be time-consuming. Aggregators like Draft2Digital, PublishDrive, and StreetLib enable you to upload your book once and then distribute it to multiple online stores, libraries, and apps.

You'll pay a fee or a percentage of sales, but in return, you save time and hassle. It's beneficial if you're going wide but don't want to juggle multiple dashboards.

Key Distribution Channels

To make an informed decision, it's essential to understand the primary distribution channels available to self-published authors.

1. Amazon KDP

Amazon KDP (Kindle Direct Publishing) is the most popular platform for self-published authors. It offers both eBook and print-on-demand services, allowing you to publish without upfront printing costs. With Amazon's global reach, your book becomes accessible to millions of readers.

2. IngramSpark

IngramSpark specialises in print-on-demand and distribution to bookstores and libraries. It's a valuable option if you want to see your book on bookstore shelves or in library catalogues. Unlike Amazon KDP, IngramSpark allows you to offer trade discounts and returns, which are essential if you want to compete with mainstream published books in physical retail settings.

. . .

3. Other Platforms

Apple Books, Google Play, Kobo, and Barnes & Noble Press are excellent platforms for reaching readers who prefer alternatives to Amazon. Each platform has its unique audience and market, providing opportunities to expand your reach.

4. Direct Sales

Selling your book directly through your website or events allows you to keep a larger share of the profits. Direct sales also create opportunities to build a deeper connection with your readers, as you can personalise signed copies or offer exclusive bundles.

5. Book Wholesalers

There's no reason why you can't use print-on-demand to sell printed books effortlessly on Amazon, whilst simultaneously using printed copies of your book to supply other retailers such as Waterstones or WH Smith. To do this effectively, you will need your book to be stocked by a major wholesaler such as Gardners, who will fulfil retailer orders on your behalf.

Combine POD and Bulk Printing for Flexibility

Print-on-demand is an excellent way to keep costs down and avoid unsold stock. But once your book starts selling steadily, it may be more cost-effective to print in bulk.

Many authors do both: they use POD to fulfil orders online, and bulk print copies for events, direct sales, or local retailers. It's a smart way to strike a balance between convenience and profit, ensuring you never run out of stock when you need it most.

The Practical Realities of Storage and Shipping

It's easy to underestimate how much space physical books take up—until 500 copies arrive on your doorstep.

If you plan to print in bulk (whether 100 or 1,000 copies), ensure you've considered where those books will be stored and how they'll be distributed. A single box of paperbacks can weigh over 10kg. Multiply that by 10 or 20 boxes, and you're talking about serious weight and volume—and severe strain on your spare room or garage.

Think about access. Can you easily get the books in and out? Will you need shelving, pallet space, or even short-term storage elsewhere?

Then there's the packaging. If you're selling directly to readers, you'll need padded envelopes or book wraps, address labels, and a method for managing postage, such as Royal Mail, couriers, or tracked or untracked services. Each has its pros and cons, particularly in terms of cost and reliability.

It's also worth factoring in your time. Packing and posting 20 orders is doable. Packing 200 can take days if you're not prepared.

Here's how to make it manageable:

- **Plan:** Before placing a bulk order, check where the books will be stored and how quickly you expect them to move.

- **Batch your fulfilment:** Group orders where possible and set aside regular "dispatch days" rather than posting ad hoc.
- **Create a system:** Even a simple spreadsheet can track orders, postage status, and follow-up emails.
- **Outsource if needed:** If storage and fulfilment become a headache, consider a fulfilment service or print-on-demand backup for specific channels.

Bulk printing can be more cost-effective per copy, but it's only a wise decision if you have a plan for getting those books into readers' hands. Distribution isn't just about access. It's about logistics.

Approaching Bookstores and Libraries

If your goal is to see your book in bookstores or libraries, there are specific steps you can take to increase your chances of success. First, ensure that your book meets professional standards in terms of editing, design, and formatting. Bookstores and libraries prioritise quality and may hesitate to stock books that appear amateurish.

For bookstores, consider offering your book on consignment, where the store pays you a percentage of the sales *after* the book is sold. Research local independent bookstores and build relationships with store managers or owners. Having a compelling pitch about why your book will resonate with their customers can make a big difference.

For libraries, tools like IngramSpark and OverDrive simplify the process of making your book available. Libraries value books that address niche interests or fill gaps in their collections, so emphasise how your book meets these needs.

Optimising Your Book for Distribution

Regardless of the channels you choose, optimising your book for distribution is essential. This includes creating an attractive and keyword-rich product description, selecting appropriate categories, and setting a competitive price. For example, your Amazon book page should highlight the unique benefits of your book while incorporating keywords that readers are likely to search for.

Additionally, offering print-on-demand options ensures your book is always available to readers without the need for significant upfront printing costs. Tools like Amazon KDP and IngramSpark make this process seamless, allowing you to focus on marketing and sales.

Design Decisions Driven by Distribution

Before you finalise your book's design, think about *where* you plan to sell it. Your distribution choices affect everything from trim size and spine width to whether you need bleed areas for illustrations.

For example, Amazon KDP offers standard trim sizes, such as 5 x 8 inches or 6 x 9 inches. IngramSpark offers additional options. If you want to sell your book through both platforms—or get stocked by bookshops—you'll need to choose a size and format that works across the board.

Balancing Reach and Effort

Deciding on your distribution strategy often comes down to striking a balance between reach and effort. If your goal is to reach the widest audience possible, wide distribution is the better choice. However, if you prefer simplicity and want to maximise the benefits of Amazon's ecosystem, exclusive distribution can be a more focused approach. Many authors find success by combining the two, starting exclusively on Amazon and later expanding to other platforms.

Understanding and choosing the proper distribution channels is a vital step in your self-publishing journey. Each option comes with its opportunities and challenges, but with careful planning and a clear understanding of your goals, you can ensure your book reaches the readers it's meant for. In the next chapter, we'll explore how to earn beyond book sales by leveraging opportunities like speaking engagements, courses, and consulting.

12

INCOME BEYOND BOOK SALES

While book sales are often the primary goal of self-publishing, they are just one of many ways to generate income from your work. A book can be a springboard to additional opportunities that not only expand your revenue streams but also establish you as an authority in your field. By thinking strategically, you can turn your book into a multi-dimensional asset that opens doors to speaking engagements, courses, consulting, and more.

This chapter explores the diverse ways self-published authors can monetise their expertise and creativity beyond traditional book sales.

Your Book as a Platform

Publishing a book establishes your credibility and creates opportunities for new ventures. A book is more than a stand-alone product; it's a tool that positions you as an expert, builds your brand, and attracts opportunities that might not otherwise come your way.

For example, a nonfiction author writing about productivity could use their book as a calling card to secure speaking engagements or to launch an online course. Similarly, a novelist might expand their storytelling into screenplays or collaborate with other creators to develop spinoff projects.

Case Study: The Power of a Platform

Here's how one author created a niche platform:

- **The Lighthouse Fanatic:** Ed is a lifelong enthusiast of lighthouses, their history and heritage. One summer, he embarked on a 3,500-mile cycle ride around the British coast, stopping to see every onshore and offshore lighthouse. His book was well publicised and has sold very well. However, the book has delivered more than just sales. In the twelve months following publications, Ed has been interviewed in magazines, newspapers, and on radio and television. If there is a media story about a lighthouse, Ed is usually contacted for a comment.

Revenue Opportunities for Authors

Once your book is published, consider these additional ways to earn from your work:

Speaking Engagements

A well-written book can make you a sought-after speaker at conferences, workshops, and corporate events. Organisers value authors because they bring unique insights and a tangible product to share with attendees. To get started, create a compelling speaker profile that highlights your book's themes and the value you bring to an audience. Reach out to event planners or list yourself on speaker bureaus to increase visibility.

Many authors find that speaking engagements not only provide income but also help sell more books. Offering signed copies at the end of your talk creates a memorable experience for attendees and a lasting connection with your message.

Courses and Workshops

If your book offers practical knowledge or inspiration, consider turning it into an online course or an in-person workshop. Platforms like Teachable, Thinkific, and Udemy make it easy to create and sell courses to a global audience. Start by identifying the key lessons or themes in your book that could be expanded into a structured learning experience.

For example, if your book is about mastering social media, you could create a course with modules on platform-specific strategies, content creation, and analytics. Workshops are another effective way to engage directly with your audience. Hosting a one-day seminar or weekend retreat based on your book allows you to charge a premium while offering personalised value.

Consulting and Coaching

Many authors, especially those in nonfiction genres, find success offering consulting or coaching services. Your book establishes your authority, and readers who connect with your message may seek one-on-one guidance to apply your expertise to their challenges.

For instance, a leadership expert might offer executive coaching, while a health and wellness author could create personalised fitness plans. These services can be provided virtually, making them accessible to clients worldwide. Use your book as a foundation to structure your services and demonstrate your expertise.

Licensing and Content Adaptation

Your book doesn't have to stay in its original format. Licensing your content for translations, audiobooks, or film adaptations can open entirely new revenue streams. Many self-published authors have found success in licensing their work for international markets, where demand for English-language books in translation is increasing.

Audiobooks are another booming market, and platforms like ACX (Audiobook Creation Exchange) make it relatively easy to create and distribute audiobooks. If your book's content is visually rich or lends itself to multimedia, consider adapting it into a webinar series, a podcast, or an interactive app.

Merchandise and Ancillary Products

If your book has a strong visual or thematic appeal, merchandise can be a fun and profitable way to expand your brand. Consider creating products like bookmarks, posters, tote bags, or mugs featuring quotes or imagery from your book. Authors of children's books might offer colouring books or plush toys based on their characters, while nonfiction authors could design planners, workbooks, or toolkits that complement their book's content.

Merchandise can be sold on your website, at events, or through platforms like Etsy, providing an additional revenue stream while deepening reader engagement.

Affiliate Marketing

If your book refers to helpful tools, platforms or resources, you might consider recommending them using affiliate links. These are special URLs that provide a small commission to you if someone purchases through your link, at no additional cost to them.

It works best when you genuinely rate the product or service. Think of it as curation rather than sales: you're helping your readers by pointing them to trusted tools, and earning a little extra at the same time.

You can include these links in blog posts, email newsletters, or on your website.

Case Studies: Thinking Beyond the Book

1. The Nonfiction Author

A business consultant used their book about leadership to create a series of online courses. The courses generated significant income and led to corporate training opportunities. The author now runs a thriving consulting and training business built around the core message of their book.

2. The Fiction Author

A fantasy novelist with a loyal fan base launched a Patreon page, offering exclusive content like bonus chapters, character art, and early access to new books. This recurring income stream not only supported their writing but also strengthened their relationship with fans.

3. The Multitasker

A wellness author created a line of branded fitness gear inspired by the message of their book. By combining book sales with merchandise and workshop revenue, they built a comprehensive brand that resonated with their audience.

Getting Started

To begin monetising beyond book sales, start by assessing the strengths of your book and your unique expertise. Ask yourself:

- What additional value can I offer readers?
- Which opportunities align with my skills and interests?
- How can I repurpose the content from my book into other formats?

Once you've identified opportunities, take small steps to test the waters. For example, host a free webinar to gauge interest in a course or reach out to local organisations to pitch yourself as a speaker. Use feedback to refine your offerings and expand over time.

Reinvesting Your Earnings

If your book starts to generate income—whether through direct sales, speaking gigs, or courses—consider reinvesting some of that profit back into your publishing plans.

That might mean hiring a publicist, commissioning professional marketing support, or funding the production of your next book. Treat your author career as a business, and carefully consider how to build and sustain momentum through your earnings.

Selling Direct Builds Trust

When you sell books directly—whether through your website or at live events—you're not just making more per copy. You're building relationships.

A signed book, a handwritten note, a face-to-face conversation—these small gestures leave a big impression. They turn casual readers into loyal fans. They make your book personal. And in a noisy market, that can be your strongest asset.

Your book is more than just a product—it's a gateway to new opportunities and revenue streams. By thinking creatively and strategically, you can transform your self-publishing success into a multifaceted career. Whether through speaking, teaching, consulting, or licensing, the possibilities are endless. In the next chapter, we'll focus on crafting a killer book launch, ensuring your book starts its journey with maximum impact.

13

CRAFTING A KILLER BOOK LAUNCH

A well-planned book launch can set the tone for your book's success, generating buzz, driving sales, and building momentum. For self-published authors, a killer launch is not just an event—it's a coordinated effort that brings your book to the attention of your target audience. A grand launch can amplify your marketing efforts, establish your brand, and create excitement among readers.

In this chapter, we'll explore the key components of a successful book launch, from planning and preparation to execution and follow-up.

Planning Your Launch

A successful book launch begins with careful planning. The earlier you start, the better prepared you'll be to handle the many moving parts involved. Begin by selecting a launch date that allows you sufficient time to prepare marketing materials, contact reviewers, and build anticipation. A lead time of at least three months is ideal.

Next, outline your launch goals. Are you focused on maximising sales during the first week? Do you want to generate reviews and word-of-mouth buzz? Perhaps your goal is to establish yourself as an authority in your niche. Defining clear objectives will guide your strategy and help you measure success.

Who's It For? Let That Guide You

Everything about your launch—where you promote it, what kind of event you host, the tone of your messaging—should reflect who your readers are. If your audience is primarily professionals, a polished LinkedIn campaign and podcast interviews may be the most effective approach. If your readers love fiction or lifestyle content, Instagram count-downs or TikTok reels might create more buzz. Start with the reader, and the tactics will follow.

Consider Offering Pre-Orders

If your platform allows it, setting up pre-orders can give your launch a head start. They help generate early sales, improve your book's ranking on release day, and create a sense of anticipation. You can also offer pre-order bonuses, such as an exclusive chapter or a free download, to reward early supporters and encourage sign-ups to your mailing list.

Building Pre-Launch Buzz

The weeks leading up to your launch are critical for creating anticipation. Start by sharing behind-the-scenes content with your audience. This could include sneak peeks at your cover design, excerpts from your book, or photos of your writing process. Use social media platforms, email newsletters, and your website to build excitement.

Advance reviews are another powerful tool for generating buzz. Reach out to bloggers, influencers, and readers who are passionate about your genre, and offer them Advance Reader Copies (ARCs) of your book. In return, ask for honest reviews to be posted on launch day or shortly after. Positive reviews can serve as social proof, encouraging others to purchase your book.

Consider hosting a countdown on your social media channels to mark the days leading up to your launch. Teasers like "5 Days to Go: Meet My Protagonist!" or "3 Days to Go: Why I Wrote This Book" keep your audience engaged and invested in your success.

Creating a Launch Day Plan

Launch day is your moment to shine, and having a detailed plan ensures everything runs smoothly. Start by announcing your book's release on all your platforms. Share a post on social media with an eye-catching graphic, send an email to your mailing list, and update your website with purchase links and a launch announcement.

To amplify your reach, consider hosting a live event. This could be a virtual book launch on Zoom, Facebook Live, or Instagram, where you talk about your book, answer questions, and share the journey behind your writing. Invite your audience to join you in celebration and include a clear call to action to purchase your book.

Exclusive launch day promotions can also drive sales. Offer a limited-time discount on your eBook or bundle it with bonus content, such as a printable workbook, a video message, or a signed bookplate. These incentives encourage readers to act quickly and reward them for supporting you.

Leveraging Post-Launch Momentum

The weeks following your launch are just as crucial as launch day itself. This is when you build on the excitement and keep your book in the spotlight. Continue to promote your book through social media, email newsletters, and collaborations with other authors or influencers.

Ask readers who have purchased your book to leave reviews on platforms like Amazon and Goodreads. Reviews play a significant role in attracting new readers and boosting your book's visibility. Make it easy for readers to leave reviews by including a friendly request at the end of your book.

You can also extend the reach of your launch by scheduling additional events. For example, host a Q&A session, participate in a podcast interview, or join an online panel related to your book's theme. These activities help maintain momentum and introduce your book to new audiences.

Build on Your Launch With Smart Follow-Up

A strong launch opens the door—but your job now is to keep readers engaged. Think about entering your book into awards, especially niche or debut author competitions. Look at your sales and traffic data to see what's working and where your readers are coming from. Offer limited-time promotions, bundle your book with extra content, or send a personal email to new subscribers. Little gestures can go a long way in turning a successful launch into lasting momentum.

Common Pitfalls to Avoid

Even the best-planned launches can encounter challenges. Here are some common pitfalls and how to avoid them:

- **Rushing the Launch:** Give yourself enough time to prepare. A rushed launch often results in missed opportunities and lower sales.
- **Neglecting Your Audience:** Stay engaged with your readers throughout the process. Respond to comments, answer questions, and show appreciation for their support.
- **Focusing Only on Sales:** While sales are significant, a successful launch also builds relationships, generates reviews, and strengthens your brand.

Case Studies: Memorable Launches

1. The Virtual Celebration

A debut author hosted a live virtual launch event, complete with giveaways and a reading of the first chapter. The event attracted several dozen attendees and led to a surge in eBook sales that evening.

2. The Niche Networker

A nonfiction author partnered with niche bloggers and podcasters in their field to promote the book. By tapping into established audiences, the launch reached a larger number of readers than expected, fostering lasting connections.

3. The Creative Campaigner

A romance writer ran a themed social media campaign, sharing quotes, artwork, and mini-stories inspired by their book. The campaign engaged followers daily in the weeks leading up to the launch, resulting in strong pre-orders.

Practical Checklist

To ensure a successful book launch, check off these essential steps:

1. Set a realistic launch date and outline your goals.
2. Create pre-launch content to build anticipation.
3. Secure advance reviews from influencers and early readers.
4. Plan a launch day event and promotional offers.
5. Follow up with post-launch activities to maintain momentum.

Crafting a killer book launch is about more than just releasing your book—it's about creating an event that captivates your audience, generates buzz, and sets the stage for long-term success. With thoughtful planning, consistent engagement, and creative promotion, your book's launch can become a decisive moment that propels your publishing journey forward. In the next chapter, we'll delve into the psychological aspects of writing and publishing, exploring how to overcome challenges and maintain motivation throughout the process.

14

THE PSYCHOLOGY OF WRITING AND PUBLISHING

The journey of writing and publishing a book is as much a mental and emotional challenge as it is a creative and technical one. Many authors grapple with self-doubt, procrastination, and the fear of failure or rejection. Even seasoned writers are not immune to these feelings. Understanding and managing the psychological aspects of writing and publishing is crucial for sustaining motivation and achieving long-term success.

In this chapter, we'll explore common psychological challenges that authors face, strategies for overcoming them, and tips for maintaining resilience throughout your self-publishing journey.

Overcoming Self-Doubt

Self-doubt is one of the most pervasive challenges authors face. Thoughts like *"Am I good enough?"* or *"Will anyone care about my book?"* can paralyse even the most confident writers.

This doubt often stems from comparing ourselves to others or fearing judgment from readers.

The first step to overcoming self-doubt is recognising that it's a natural part of the creative process. Every author, no matter how successful, has experienced it at some point. Instead of letting doubt stop you, use it as an opportunity to reflect and grow. Remind yourself of your unique voice and the value your book brings to the world. Remember, there is no one else who can tell your story the way you can.

Affirmations and positive self-talk can also be helpful. Reframe negative thoughts by focusing on your progress and strengths. For instance, replace *"I'm not a real writer"* with *"I'm learning and improving every day."* Surrounding yourself with supportive people, such as a writing group or mentor, can provide encouragement and perspective when doubt creeps in.

It's Normal to Feel Exposed

Publishing a book—especially your first—can feel oddly exposing. You're not just sharing ideas or stories; you're sharing something of yourself. That can make you feel vulnerable, even after you've done everything 'right.'

But here's the truth: vulnerability isn't a weakness. It's proof that you care. It means your book matters to you, and that passion is what makes it worth reading.

Managing Procrastination

Procrastination is another common challenge, often fueled by perfectionism or fear of failure. It's easy to put off writing when the task feels overwhelming or when you're unsure of how to begin.

The key to managing procrastination is breaking your work into smaller, manageable tasks. Instead of focusing on completing an entire chapter, set a goal to write 300 words or outline a single section. These smaller steps make the process less intimidating and help you build momentum.

Establishing a routine can also be transformative. Set aside dedicated time each day or week to write and treat it as non-negotiable. Creating a distraction-free environment—whether it's a quiet room, a library, or a local café—can help you stay focused. If you struggle with accountability, consider partnering with a fellow writer to share progress and goals.

Manage Your Expectations

At some point in the journey, you might ask yourself: "Is it worth it?" Maybe you're tired. Maybe progress feels slow. Perhaps you pictured your launch going differently.

It helps to come back to your expectations. Were they realistic? Were they your own, or borrowed from someone else's highlight reel?

The road to publishing is rarely smooth, but that doesn't mean you're doing it wrong.

Dealing with Criticism and Rejection

No matter how much effort you put into your book, not everyone will love it. Criticism and rejection are inevitable parts of the writing journey, and learning to handle them constructively is essential for growth.

When faced with criticism, take a moment to distinguish between constructive feedback and unhelpful negativity. Constructive criticism, such as a reviewer suggesting ways to tighten your plot or clarify your arguments, can be a valuable tool for improvement. On the other hand, ignore remarks that are simply mean-spirited or provide nothing useful to improve your work.

Rejection is similarly common, particularly for authors who pitch their books to traditional publishers or agents. Instead of viewing rejection as a reflection of your worth, see it as a stepping stone to success. Many best-selling authors, from J.K. Rowling to Stephen King, faced multiple rejections before finding their breakthrough. Keep refining your craft and pursuing opportunities, knowing that every "no" brings you closer to a "yes."

From Gatekeeping to Empowerment

Traditional publishing has long relied on gatekeepers—agents, editors, marketing teams—deciding whose stories get told. For many writers, this has meant years of rejection, near misses, or simply never feeling like their work fits the mould.

Self-publishing changes that.

It hands the power back to you, the author. You decide if your book is ready. You choose your editor, your cover designer, and your publication date. You're not waiting for permission—you're building a path for yourself.

That can feel thrilling. But it can also feel daunting. When you remove the gatekeepers, you remove the buffers. There's no one else to validate your work. No industry stamp of approval. And that can stir up all sorts of doubts.

Here's the truth: choosing to self-publish doesn't mean your book wasn't good enough for a publisher. It means you've chosen a different route—one that prioritises autonomy, speed, creative control, and reader connection over industry norms.

It means you're taking yourself seriously.

And that shift—from hoping to be chosen, to choosing yourself—is a powerful act of self-belief. It's not just about publishing. It's about claiming space, owning your story, and trusting your voice.

Building Resilience

Writing and publishing are long-term endeavours, and resilience is key to staying the course. Resilience isn't about avoiding setbacks—it's about bouncing back from them with determination and a renewed sense of purpose.

One way to build resilience is to celebrate small wins along the way. Writing a chapter, hitting a word count goal, or receiving positive feedback from a beta reader are all achievements worth acknowledging. These milestones remind you of the progress you're making and keep you motivated.

Another strategy is to focus on your "why." Reflect on why you started writing your book and the impact you hope it will have on your readers. Keeping your purpose at the forefront helps you push through challenges and stay committed to your goals.

Finally, don't underestimate the importance of self-care. Writing is mentally and emotionally demanding, so it's essential to take time to recharge. Take breaks, exercise regularly, and spend quality time with loved ones to maintain balance and prevent burnout.

Celebrate Your Progress

Finished a chapter? Sent a draft to a beta reader? Hit your word count three days in a row? Celebrate it.

Small wins matter. They build momentum and remind you that you're moving forward—even when it doesn't feel like it.

Don't wait for launch day to feel proud. You're already doing something bold and brilliant, and each step is worth acknowledging.

The Role of Community

Writing can be a solitary activity, but you don't have to go through it alone. Joining a community of writers can provide invaluable support, encouragement, and accountability. Whether it's an online forum, a local writing group, or a critique circle, connecting with others who understand your journey can make the process less isolating.

Communities also offer opportunities for learning and growth. Sharing your work with others allows you to receive feedback, discover new perspectives, and refine your craft.

Likewise, supporting fellow writers fosters a sense of camaraderie and mutual success.

Case Studies: Authors Who Overcame Challenges

1. The Persistent Novelist

A debut novelist struggled with self-doubt and nearly abandoned their manuscript. After joining a critique group and receiving encouragement from their peers, they completed and self-published their first book, which received positive reviews. The support of a community helped them believe in their work and take the leap.

2. The Procrastinating Professional

A non-fiction author juggled writing with a demanding full-time job. By breaking their project into small, manageable tasks and dedicating just 30 minutes a day to writing, they finished their book within six months. Consistency, even in small doses, proved to be the key to success.

3. The Resilient Memoirist

A memoirist faced rejection from multiple publishers but decided to self-publish instead. Their book resonated with readers, leading to speaking engagements and media coverage. Rather than giving up, they adapted their strategy and found success on their terms.

The psychological aspects of writing and publishing can be challenging, but they are also opportunities for growth and self-discovery. By addressing self-doubt, managing procrastination, and building resilience, you can overcome obstacles and stay motivated throughout your journey. Writing a book is an accomplishment in itself, and navigating the ups and downs with courage and perseverance will make the experience all the more rewarding.

In the next chapter, we'll explore how to navigate reviews and reader feedback, ensuring you handle praise and criticism with professionalism and grace.

15

NAVIGATING REVIEWS AND READER FEEDBACK

Once your book is published, it enters the hands of readers, and with that comes feedback in the form of reviews, ratings, and direct responses. Reviews can be both exhilarating and daunting. Positive feedback validates your hard work, while negative reviews or criticism can feel personal and discouraging. However, navigating reviews and reader feedback is an essential skill for every author, as it helps you grow, build credibility, and maintain a professional image.

In this chapter, we'll explore strategies for encouraging reviews, handling criticism constructively, and leveraging reader feedback to strengthen your future work.

The Importance of Reviews

Reviews play a critical role in your book's success. They provide social proof, helping potential readers decide whether your book is worth their time and money. On platforms like Amazon, Goodreads, and Apple Books, books with a higher number of reviews are more likely to appear in search results, increasing visibility.

Reviews are especially important for self-published authors, as readers often rely on them in the absence of traditional publishing endorsements. A robust collection of reviews signals that your book has been read and appreciated, which builds trust and attracts new readers.

Encouraging Readers to Leave Reviews

To encourage readers to leave reviews, a proactive approach is necessary. Most readers won't leave a review unless prompted, so it's essential to make the process as easy and inviting as possible.

One effective strategy is to include a polite review request at the end of your book. For example, you might write, *"Thank you for reading! If you enjoyed this book, please consider leaving a review on Amazon or Goodreads. Your feedback helps other readers discover this book and supports independent authors like me."* This simple addition can significantly increase the like-lihood of reviews.

You can also engage directly with your readers on social media or through email newsletters. Share posts about how much reviews mean to you and your writing journey, and encourage readers to share their thoughts. Offering a small incentive, such as entry into a giveaway for a free signed copy or exclusive content, can further motivate readers to leave feedback.

If you have an Advanced Reader Copy (ARC) program, use it to build momentum before your book's launch. Reach out to bloggers, influencers, and early readers who enjoy your genre and offer them an advance reader copy (ARC) in exchange for an honest review. Be sure to follow up with gentle reminders in the days leading up to your launch date.

Avoid Paying for Reviews

It may be tempting to expedite the process by paying for reviews. Don't. Not only does it break the rules of most platforms, but it also erodes reader trust. Today's readers are sharp. They can spot a manufactured review a mile off. Focus instead on earning authentic reviews from people who've genuinely connected with your book.

Handling Negative Reviews

Negative reviews are an inevitable part of publishing, and they can be challenging to handle. It's natural to feel hurt or defensive when someone criticises your work, but it's essential to approach negative reviews with professionalism and grace.

First, remind yourself that reviews are subjective. Not every book is for every reader, and a negative review often reflects personal preferences rather than a flaw in your work. Resist the urge to respond directly to negative reviews, especially in a public forum. Engaging with critical reviewers can escalate tensions and may harm your reputation.

Instead, use constructive criticism to improve your craft. If multiple readers mention the same issue, such as pacing or character development, consider it an opportunity to reflect and grow as a writer. However, not all criticism is constructive—learn to filter out unhelpful comments and focus on feedback that aligns with your goals.

Sort the Signal from the Noise

Not every review deserves equal weight. Some readers will offer thoughtful, actionable feedback, while others will vent their frustrations. Learn to tell the difference. Constructive criticism often highlights patterns, such as pacing issues or underdeveloped characters. That's useful. But if someone didn't "get" your book or wasn't your audience, you don't need to take it to heart.

Leveraging Positive Reviews

Positive reviews are invaluable for marketing and building your brand. When readers praise your book, their words carry more weight than your promotional efforts. Highlight positive reviews on your website, social media, or marketing materials. For example, you can create a graphic featuring a glowing quote from a reader or share a post expressing gratitude for the kind words.

Reach out to readers who leave particularly enthusiastic reviews and thank them personally, if appropriate. Building a relationship with your most passionate fans can lead to word-of-mouth recommendations and long-term support for your work.

Engaging with Reader Feedback

Reader feedback isn't limited to formal reviews—it can also come through emails, social media messages, or in-person interactions. Engaging with readers who take the time to share their thoughts fosters a sense of connection and loyalty.

Respond to positive feedback with genuine appreciation. For instance, if a reader messages you to say they loved your book, thank them warmly and, if possible, ask what resonated with them most. This not only shows you value their input but also provides insights into what aspects of your writing connect with your audience.

For constructive criticism shared directly, approach the conversation with an open mind. Readers who offer thoughtful feedback often want to help you improve, not tear you down. Thank them for their honesty and consider their suggestions carefully.

Look for Patterns—and Act on Them

If multiple readers raise the same issue—whether it's about clarity, flow, or tone—pay attention. These patterns reveal where your book might not be landing as you intended. You may even decide to update the book or adapt your approach next time. Don't see it as failure—it's a sign that your work is being read, understood, and taken seriously.

Case Studies: Authors Navigating Reviews

1. The Grateful Memoirist

A memoirist included a heartfelt request for reviews at the end of their book, explaining how much feedback meant to them as an independent author. This personal touch resonated with readers, resulting in a steady stream of positive reviews that boosted visibility.

2. The Resilient Fiction Writer

A novelist received criticism about the pacing of their debut book. Instead of taking it personally, they used the feedback to refine the structure of their next manuscript. The result was a more substantial sophomore effort that earned praise for its compelling narrative flow.

3. The Social Media Savvy Nonfiction Author

A nonfiction author created a recurring "Review Spotlight" series on Instagram, sharing quotes from positive reviews alongside a thank-you message. This strategy not only celebrated their readers but also encouraged others to leave reviews.

Practical Tips for Managing Reviews

- Include a polite request for feedback in your book to encourage readers to provide their thoughts.
- Use an ARC program to generate reviews before your book's launch.
- Focus on the constructive aspects of criticism and let go of unhelpful negativity.
- Highlight positive reviews in your marketing to build credibility and attract new readers.
- Engage with readers who share feedback, showing appreciation and fostering connections.

Navigating reviews and reader feedback is an integral part of the self-publishing journey. By encouraging reviews, handling criticism with professionalism, and capitalising on positive feedback, you can enhance your reputation, foster meaningful connections with readers, and grow as an author. Remember, every review, positive or negative, is a sign that your book is reaching an audience, and that in itself is a significant accomplishment.

Congratulations on making it this far — that alone sets you apart.

You now have a clear, honest roadmap for turning your ideas into a finished book you can be proud of. You know how to spot the traps, avoid the false promises, and make smart choices every step of the way — from first draft to final sale.

Remember: self-publishing isn't about rushing it out and hoping for the best. It's about doing it properly, on your terms, with your reader in mind. Take your time. Revisit these pages when you need a reminder. Stay focused on why you started, and keep your reader at the heart of every decision you make.

Most importantly, get started. Decide on your next step today, no matter how small. Write the next page. Tweak your plan. Reach out to an editor. Momentum builds confidence, and confidence finishes books.

And if you'd like straight-talking, practical support as you put your plan into action, join me for one of my live online courses at:

https://www.getpublished.tv

No jargon. No hype. Just real guidance for real writers — delivered by someone who's been where you are and knows what works.

Your book matters. You're ready. Now make it happen.

Ed.

16

RESOURCES FOR UK AUTHORS

There are hundreds of UK organisations, websites and other resources whose aim is to help you succeed as a self-published author. From obtaining professional support to finding promotional opportunities, taking advantage of them can make your publishing journey smoother and more rewarding. This section provides an expanded list of practical names, addresses, and websites, tailored to the UK publishing landscape.

Publishing Essentials: ISBNs

To make your book widely available, obtaining an ISBN is essential.

Nielsen ISBN Agency for UK & Ireland

Buy single ISBNs or blocks for multiple books. Includes registration in Nielsen's industry databases.

- https://www.nielsenisbnstore.com
- Contact: 01483 712 215

Legal Deposit

All UK publishers are legally required to deposit one copy of every published book with the British Library.

The British Library

- https://www.bl.uk/legal-deposit
- Notes: You may also be asked to deposit copies with other legal deposit libraries, such as Oxford's Bodleian Library or Cambridge University Library.

Professional Organisations and Networks

The Society of Authors (SoA)

A UK-based organisation that supports authors with legal advice, advocacy, and networking opportunities.

- https://www.societyofauthors.org
- Membership Fee: A sliding scale based on income, starting at £112 per annum.

The Alliance of Independent Authors (ALLi)

A global organisation with strong UK representation, focusing on self-publishing best practices.

- https://www.allianceindependentauthors.org

- Services: Educational resources, discounts on publishing tools, and a community forum.

Spread the Word

A London-based organisation supporting writers through workshops, mentoring, and networking events.

- https://www.spreadtheword.org.uk
- Notes: Focuses on emerging voices and diverse communities.

Specialised Support for Indie Authors

The Self-Publishing Partnership (SPP)

Provides services for authors who need help with editing, design, and production.

- https://www.selfpublishingpartnership.co.uk

Indie Author Support Groups

The UK Self-Publishing Group (Facebook):

A vibrant online community offering advice and camaraderie.

The Writing Grotto:

A supportive writing network that organises workshops and critiques.

Editing, Design, and Production

The Chartered Institute of Editing and Proofreading (CIEP)

- https://www.ciep.uk
- Notes: Directory of professional editors in the UK.

Cover Design and Typesetting

99designs:

- Platform for professional cover design.
- https://99designs.co.uk

Design for Writers:

A UK-based design service specialising in book covers and interiors.

- https://www.designforwriters.com

Digital and Litho Printing

Short Run Press

- 25 Bittern Road, Exeter, EX2 7LW
- Phone: 01392 211909
- E-mail: estimates@shortrunpress.co.uk

Clays Ltd. (Part of the CPI Group)

A long-standing UK printer offering large-scale print runs for authors.

- https://www.clays.co.uk

Marketing and Promotion

LoveReading

- https://www.lovereading.co.uk
- Notes: Includes promotional packages for indie authors

BookMachine

Networking and training for authors and publishing professionals.

- https://bookmachine.org

Events and Book Fairs

London Book Fair

Offers indie author programs and networking opportunities.

- https://www.londonbookfair.co.uk

The Self-Publishing Show Live

A UK-based conference focused on self-publishing.

- https://selfpublishingformula.com/spslive

Financial Assistance and Grants

Arts Council England

Provides funding for authors working on creative projects.

- https://www.artscouncil.org.uk

The Royal Literary Fund

Supports professional writers facing financial hardship.

- https://www.rlf.org.uk

Creative Scotland (for authors in Scotland)

- https://www.creativescotland.com

Collecting Secondary Royalties

If your work is ever photocopied, shared digitally, or used in educational or broadcast contexts, you may be entitled to secondary royalties. The Authors' Licensing and Collecting Society (ALCS) collects these payments on behalf of UK writers. Registering is straightforward, and it's one of the few areas where money might arrive out of the blue. Well worth doing.

https://www.alcs.co.uk

Useful Online Tools and Resources

The Writers' & Artists' Yearbook

Directory of industry contacts and practical publishing advice.

- https://www.writersandartists.co.uk

British Council Literature

Resources for authors seeking international opportunities.

- https://literature.britishcouncil.org

ProWritingAid

A powerful tool for editing and improving writing.

- https://prowritingaid.com

Libraries and Academic Resources

Public Lending Rights (PLR) UK

Authors can earn royalties when their books are borrowed from UK libraries.

- https://www.bl.uk/plr

The British Council Library

Provides authors with access to a global audience and resources.

- https://library.britishcouncil.org

Looking Beyond the UK

While this section focuses on UK-specific support, your potential readership is global. Platforms like Amazon KDP and Draft2Digital allow you to publish internationally. Online events, freelance professionals, and international collaborations can help your book reach a wider audience. Consider attending virtual book fairs, pitching to global podcasts, or collaborating with authors from other countries. The world's never been more open to indie publishing.

These additional resources ensure UK self-published authors have a comprehensive toolkit to succeed at every stage of their journey. Whether you're seeking expert guidance, funding, or marketing platforms, these contacts provide the foundation to achieve your publishing goals.

READY TO REALLY GET STARTED?

Reading this book is a brilliant start, but publishing your book doesn't happen on paper alone.

If you'd like step-by-step help to publish your book sooner (and with fewer headaches), join me for my online Self-Publishing training programme, delivered online LIVE over five afternoons.

- Live, practical sessions — not pre-recorded videos.
- No jargon, no false promises — just honest guidance from a publishing sector expert.
- Small group support — Maximum of 12 writers on each course.
- Walk away with a clear plan, ready to publish.

Book readers get a special bonus: When you join from this book, you'll also receive my exclusive companion workbook to help you put every lesson into action.

Find out more and secure your place at:
www.getpublished.tv/courses/self-publish-properly

I can't wait to help you make your book a reality.

Ed.

www.ingramcontent.com/pod-product-compliance
Lightning Source LLC
Chambersburg PA
CBHW071222090426
42736CB00014B/2940